BI
Be   1956-

D0651733

JAN 2 7 2005

BOOK "MARKS"

If you wish to keep a record that you have
read this book, you may use spaces
below to mark a private code. Please do
not mark the book in any other way.

Sam 6	ⱳ Ä ≔	⸝⸝		

Thomas Jefferson

The Revolution of Ideas

OXFORD
PORTRAITS

Thomas Jefferson

The Revolution of Ideas

R. B. Bernstein

OXFORD
UNIVERSITY PRESS

*To the memory of my father, Fred Bernstein, who will
always live in my heart, and to my b'sheret, Danielle J. Lewis,
whose faith in me never wavers and who taught me to believe
in second chances.*

OXFORD
UNIVERSITY PRESS

Oxford New York
Auckland Bangkok Buenos Aires Cape Town Chennai
Dar es Salaam Delhi Hong Kong Istanbul Karachi Kolkata
Kuala Lumpur Madrid Melbourne Mexico City Mumbai
Nairobi São Paulo Shanghai Taipei Tokyo Toronto

Published by Oxford University Press, Inc.
198 Madison Avenue, New York, New York 10016
www.oup.com

Design: Greg Wozney
Layout: Alexis Siroc

Library of Congress Cataloging-in-Publication Data
Bernstein, R. B., 1956–
Thomas Jefferson: the revolution of ideas / R. B. Bernstein.
p. cm. — (Oxford portraits)
Includes bibliographical references and index.
ISBN 0-19-514368-X (alk. paper)
1. Jefferson, Thomas, 1743–1826—Juvenile literature. 2. Presidents—
United States—Biography—Juvenile literature. 3. Jefferson, Thomas, 1743–1826—
Political and social views—Juvenile literature. 4. United States—Politics and
government—1775–1783—Juvenile literature. 5. United States—Politics and
government—1783–1865—Juvenile literature. I. Title. II. Series.
E332.79 .B47 2003
973.4'6'092—dc22

2003017866

9 8 7 6 5 4 3 2 1

Printed in the United States of America on acid-free paper

On the cover: Thomas Jefferson by Rembrandt Peale, 1805
Frontispiece: Bust of Thomas Jefferson by Jean-Antoine Houdon, 1789

CONTENTS

could the dead feel any interest in Monu-ments or other remembrances of them, when, as Anacreon says Ολιγη δε κεισομεϑα Κονις, οστεων λυϑεντων the following would be to my Manes the most gratifying.

On the grave a plain die or cube of 3.f without any mouldings, surmounted by an Obelisk of 6.f. height, each of a single stone: on the faces of the Obelisk the following inscription, & not a word more

"Here was buried
Thomas Jefferson
Author of the Declaration of American Independance
of the Statute of Virginia for religious freedom
& Father of the University of Virginia."

because by these, as testimonials that I have lived, I wish most to be remembered. to be of the coarse stone of which my columns are made, that no one might be tempted hereafter to destroy it for the value of the materials. my bust by Ciracchi, with the pedestal and truncated column on which it stands, might be given to the University if they would place it in the Dome room of the Rotunda. on the Die of the Obelisk might be engraved

Born Apr. 2. 1743. O.S.
Died ———

Always meticulous about his efforts to shape his historical reputation, Jefferson designed his tombstone and composed his epitaph in early 1826, months before his death.

Introduction

As you stand before the family cemetery at Monticello, separated from the tree-shaded graveyard by a plain iron fence, the central tombstone draws your gaze. An obelisk of gray stone, it bears a simple inscription:

HERE WAS BURIED
THOMAS JEFFERSON
APRIL 2, 1743 O.S.—JULY 4, 1826
AUTHOR OF THE DECLARATION
OF INDEPENDENCE
AND OF THE VIRGINIA STATUTE FOR
RELIGIOUS FREEDOM,
AND THE FATHER OF THE UNIVERSITY
OF VIRGINIA.

Today's monument was erected in the 1880s to replace the original, which had weathered badly—due in part to the souvenir lust of generations of visitors armed with pocketknives. The inscription, however, is the same one that Thomas Jefferson composed in the last year of his life, listing the achievements "by which," he wrote, "I most wish to be remembered."

The cemetery is a peaceful place. The tourists who descend on it become silent as they approach the fence. That silence is not only what Jefferson had in mind for his grave, but also what he craved in life. He always claimed to yearn for a life of tranquil contemplation, spent with his books, his architectural drawings, and his researches in science.

In life, however, Jefferson never found the quiet that surrounds him in death. As a politician and statesman, he was embroiled in controversy, subjected to waves of criticism and ridicule, wounded so often and so deeply that he never recovered. Perhaps for this reason he omitted his political offices from his epitaph. The words he chose, however, are as notable for what they say as for what they leave out. Jefferson presented himself to future generations as a man concerned above all with ideas. That is the common theme linking the three achievements he listed on his tombstone.

He first claimed authorship of the American Revolution's central political testament, the most eloquent statement of the new nation's core principles and of a dream that has swept the world—independence and self-government. He next declared himself author of his era's most revolutionary statute, which denied government the authority to dictate what men and women should believe in matters of religion. Finally, he proclaimed himself father of a university allied with no religion or church, a home for the life of the mind that would foster an educated population, serve his beloved Virginia, and be a model to the world. In sum, Jefferson wanted posterity to see him as he saw himself, as spokesman of a revolution of ideas that would make the world over again.

Independence, self-government, religious liberty, and an enlightened citizenry are key stars of Jefferson's constellation of revolutionary ideas; they still attract our gaze and illuminate our hopes. There are other stars in Jefferson's constellation, however, that shone brightly for him but have faded for us.

One was Jefferson's vision of the good society as a republic of independent farmers. Self-sufficient to the greatest possible degree, they would maintain their virtuously simple lives and thus preserve the republic. They would feel no cravings for wealth and luxury, or for the economic activities (trade and commerce) that create and distribute them.

Another star in Jefferson's intellectual constellation was his idea of the nature of the American Union. Jefferson was both a passionate nationalist and an equally enthusiastic believer that each state had to be as independent as possible within a limited federal republic. Over time, he developed an elaborate picture of the ideal structure of American politics and government. It took the form of a pyramid. At the base were the wards, the local subdivisions within which Virginians and other Americans would govern themselves. Above the wards were counties, and above them were the states, which Jefferson saw as the true units of American government. The federal government, with limited powers for limited purposes, was the pyramid's capstone.

A third now-eclipsed star was Jefferson's idea of who could be citizens of his federal republic. Jefferson did not welcome modern visions of a multicultural, multiracial society. He was willing to include Native American peoples in his vision of America, but only if they gave up their traditional ways and cultures and embraced the agricultural way of life that he insisted was the only true basis of a good society. Otherwise, they would have to leave the United States. Jefferson's view of slavery was deeply conflicted, but his view of enslaved people of African descent, and even of free African Americans, was not.

Believing that natural rights were gifts of God to any human being who had the ability to tell right from wrong, Jefferson regarded slavery with anguish and despair. And yet that anguish and despair hardened his belief that, even if slavery were abolished, the freed slaves could not live side-by-side with their former masters. He feared that relations between former slaves and former masters would be bitter and angry, and he believed that people of African descent were inferior to whites. Jefferson's views about race grew stronger as he became older; his early antislavery views faded and he grew more convinced that white Americans faced an insoluble dilemma. In 1820, he wrote about this dilemma in memorable terms to the Massachusetts politician John Holmes: "We have the wolf by the ears, and we can neither hold him, nor safely let him go. Justice is in one scale, and self-preservation in the other."

Finally, Jefferson was haunted by the specter of debt, which overshadowed his lands and his life. To Jefferson, debt was the greatest threat to personal and national independence. His own debts ate away at his ability to live his life as he pleased and saddled him with obligations to others that he tried but failed to meet. He saw national debt as a death sentence for a free republic, for debt caused corruption and war, and corruption and war would destroy American liberty. In the end, debt shattered Jefferson's hopes for himself and for the United States. His own debts destroyed his dream of passing Monticello to his heirs; American debts doomed his vision of the self-sufficient, uncorrupted republic of farmers he had fought to create.

Jefferson had a deep personal stake in this revolution of ideas. Other Americans shared his commitment to that revolution, but with varying levels of enthusiasm and with differing ideas in mind. Jefferson was almost alone in the strength and passion of his commitment to one crowning idea: that this revolution was universal. He saw the American Revolution as the first chapter of an age of democratic revolution that would sweep all of humanity. By contrast, his old friend and sometime ally John Adams believed that the American Revolution was an American event only, without larger world significance.

Jefferson's belief that the Revolution was universal had its limits. He was not inclined to extend it to women, nor to Native Americans who insisted on following their traditional ways, nor to African Americans. Even so, the universalism at the core of his revolution of ideas transcended his hopes and expectations, in the process nourishing and spreading his reputation as a philosopher and defender of liberty.

The contradictions of Jefferson's life bedevil all who study him. Jefferson was an advocate of liberty who owned slaves; he became a troubled apologist for slavery, justifying it by racial theories that, he claimed, were based on science. He was a champion of limited government who wanted power to rest with the states, but as President he devised creative, expansive uses of national power—in some cases bordering on the tyrannical. He was a private man who claimed to loathe politics, but he became his era's dominant politician. He was a man of aristocratic habits and tastes who became a symbol of American democracy and its most eloquent voice. He was a cultivated Virginia gentleman of the late 18th century, but he became a timeless theorist of liberty, democracy, and the rights of man.

The range of Jefferson's interests and pursuits was amazing even in a time when all knowledge seemed open to anyone who wanted to absorb it. Jefferson was an eager participant in the intellectual world of the Enlightenment, that vast and varied body of ideas and arguments that dominated the Western world for more than a century, and he let his mind range far and wide. He was a talented architect, a skilled violinist, a bold student of religion, a devoted amateur scientist and sponsor of scientific research, a connoisseur of food and wine, an enthusiastic tinkerer who loved to adapt and improve upon inventions, and perhaps the finest writer of his time. The problem is that, too often, Jefferson gets credit for originality that he did not claim or deserve. Although widely read and energetically curious, he was a brilliant adapter and interpreter of his era's ideas rather than a figure of towering creativity.

Jefferson's private life was interwoven with his careers as politician and thinker. He was not a solitary philosopher-politician—he was also a planter, slaveholder, husband, father, and lover. Jefferson tried to sort his life into tidy compartments, but his public and private selves inevitably spilled over the edges and blended together. One area of spillover examined in recent scholarship is Jefferson's relationship with his slave Sally Hemings, an issue that has sparked agonized controversy.

Jefferson poses many challenges for anyone who would write his life. One challenge is that there is so much to fit into a coherent frame. He wrote at least 16,000 letters, and received at least 26,000. Not only did he write more than perhaps any other American of his time, but he also wrote more extensively and brilliantly than any of them, seeming to display his thoughts and feelings on the page. Yet he mostly showed himself as he wanted to be seen. Jefferson was a guarded, deeply private man who presented a series of versions of himself to friends, colleagues, admirers, and adversaries; he rarely showed the self-criticism or self-knowledge that we find, for example, in John Adams's writings. We must work by indirection, sifting tantalizingly cryptic clues, looking beneath the surface of his words for meanings that he might not have known were there. Jefferson was a human kaleidoscope; the elements of his thought and character assume different patterns and shadings from encounter to encounter, crisis to crisis, moment to moment.

Jefferson's character has always been an issue. Throughout his life, and in the nearly two centuries since his death, he has been charged with dishonesty. Sometimes he said and did different things because his ideas changed over time. For example, he based his vision of a good society on agriculture, which he saw as the most virtuous way of life, but he himself experimented with manufacturing, founding a grist mill and a nail factory at Monticello (and hoping to make a profit from them).

Sometimes his inconsistencies are clues to deep differences in values between his era and ours. For example, he claimed to hate politics but allowed his name to be put forward for high political office. Was he dishonest? Or was he acting as a gentleman of his era would, knowing that naked ambition was dishonorable and that a candidate was supposed to deny ambition and to accept office reluctantly? In a more troubling example, his arguments for human equality clash with his opinions about racial inequality and about the differences that he said fitted men for, but should exclude women from, politics and government. He defended freedoms of speech and press, but he was willing to use harsh legal measures against those who attacked him or disputed his views of democracy. He could voice friendship for someone, but criticize him harshly to others. Jefferson knew so many people that he could write conflicting things to different people with slight risk that the inconsistencies would emerge in his lifetime. When those conflicts did surface, he found the resulting uproar deeply embarrassing.

In recent years, Americans have grown to distrust those who claim to speak in the name of the people; they are cynical about politicians and suspicious of government. Jefferson's words have fueled such views of government and politics. Ironically, many people apply their distrust, cynicism, and suspicion to Jefferson himself, often reacting against the hero-worship formerly lavished on him.

Jefferson was a key figure in creating the idea that the United States was safe from any danger from abroad—an idea shattered by the September 11, 2001, tragedies. On March 4, 1801, in his first Presidential inaugural address, he reminded his countrymen that they were "[k]indly separated by nature and a wide ocean from the exterminating havoc of one quarter of the globe. . . ." What the Japanese attack on Pearl Harbor in 1941 could not do, what nearly half a century of the cold war could not do, the events of September 11 did. The destruction of the World Trade Center, the attack on the Pentagon, and the crash of Flight 93 in rural Pennsylvania combined to end once and for all the idea that the United States is safe from physical attack.

In this new and frightening world, we might ask, what relevance does the life of Thomas Jefferson have for us?

Politicians and commentators tell us that we live in an era of unprecedented crisis. And yet Jefferson and his contemporaries lived their entire adult lives in an atmosphere of constant crisis. From 1765 to 1775, they had to weather the dispute with Great Britain over the American colonists' rights and responsibilities within the British Empire. From 1775 through 1783, they had to declare and win American independence in a grueling war against one of the world's greatest military and naval powers. Beginning in 1776, they launched a series of unprecedented struggles to invent new forms of government to preserve the liberty they would win in that Revolution. Even after they adopted the Constitution in 1788, their sense of crisis was not at an end. Now they faced yet another series of struggles, spanning the rest of their lives, to make their new systems and institutions of government work, to conduct politics within a new and untried constitutional framework, to test whether political conflict and factional strife could be contained within the matrix of the Constitution. Even in retirement, Jefferson, Madison, and their colleagues were besieged by questions, pleas, and demands for advice and guidance.

Jefferson and his contemporaries always were aware how fragile these experiments in government were, and that awareness fed their sense of crisis. They were committed to preserving the American Republic, and they were willing to pay a high price for that commitment. Their devotion to these ideals ought to reassure us—and to challenge us. Jefferson and the other members of the Revolutionary generation had to learn on the run, and their most remarkable exercises of creative adaptation should challenge us to do likewise.

A note on quotations: Jefferson and his contemporaries wrote before the standardization of spelling, capitalization, and punctuation. Thus, all quotations appear as they do in their original sources.

A YOUNG GENTLEMAN OF VIRGINIA (1743–1774)

Thomas Jefferson told his children and grandchildren that his earliest memory was of a trusted slave carrying him, at the age of two, on a pillow when his family moved from his birthplace, the Shadwell plantation, to the Tuckahoe plantation, along the James River above Richmond, Virginia. Eighty-one years later, in 1826, as Jefferson lay on his deathbed, another trusted slave obeyed his dying request to have his pillows adjusted so that he could lie more comfortably. From cradle to grave, Jefferson was surrounded and supported by the institution of slavery, a core element of the life of Virginia's gentlemen farmers. No matter how modern, even forward-looking, he seems to us, he was a product of his time and place.

Jefferson, a member of one of Virginia's most prominent families, was born and raised on the western edge of Great Britain's American empire. His early makeup thus blended aristocrat and frontiersman. He was born in April 1743 at Shadwell, in Goochland (later Albemarle) County. He recorded his birth date as April 2, 1743, under the "Old Style" (the "O.S." referred to in the inscription on his tombstone) calendar used in England until 1758. When in that year the British adopted the more reliable Gregorian calendar, all dates shifted forward 11 days; thus, we observe Jefferson's birthday on April 13.

Jefferson's mother, Jane Randolph Jefferson, born in 1720, was one of the wealthy, proud Randolphs, the most numerous family in Virginia's planter elite. The Randolphs claimed to be descended from the royal houses of England and Scotland—claims that Jefferson dismissed as arrogant and pointless. We know almost nothing about Jane Randolph Jefferson. No letters between her and her son survive, and the few surviving references to her in his papers are cold and matter-of-fact.

By contrast, Jefferson was proud of his father. Born in 1708, a descendant of immigrants from Wales, Peter Jefferson won fame and respect for his industry, strength, endurance, and skill as a surveyor and mapmaker. In 1751, with Joshua Fry, he surveyed Virginia and prepared the first accurate map of the province. Thomas Jefferson proudly reprinted his father's map in his only book, *Notes on the State of Virginia* (1787). As an old man, he told his grandchildren stories of his father's heroic feats. For example, according to tradition, Peter once ordered his slaves to pull down a building on his plantation. When they confessed that they could not do it, he seized the rope and, with one mighty pull, brought it down himself.

Unlike Alexander Hamilton, whose brilliance as a child attracted the attention of his admiring elders, the young Thomas Jefferson is a shadowy figure. All we have are stories of his upbringing that he told his children and grandchildren. He had two older sisters, one younger brother, and two younger sisters. One older sister, Elizabeth, suffered from some form of mental retardation. In early 1774, at the age of 28, she wandered from the family house during a thunderstorm and was found dead after the storm. The few letters of Jefferson's younger brother, Randolph, suggest that he was, at most, of average intelligence. One thing we know about the young Jefferson is that, by the age of nine, he already enjoyed music and could play the violin; he often accompanied his adored older sister Jane when she sang.

Self-made and self-taught, Peter Jefferson valued education, and he inspired a similar love of learning in his oldest son. Because colonial Virginia had no public schools, gentleman farmers hired private tutors to teach their children. Thus, the very young Thomas Jefferson was tutored at home. When Thomas was nine, Peter enrolled him in a local private school run by the Reverend William Douglas. Douglas taught Latin and Greek, the basis of a gentleman's education. Although Thomas took to the classical languages easily, he did not like Douglas and thought little of his abilities.

In 1757, when Thomas was 14, Peter Jefferson died at the age of 49. His will named two friends to oversee the family's finances and serve as guardians for the children. They found Thomas a new tutor, the Reverend James Maury. In his autobiography, Jefferson called Maury a "correct classical scholar," which, for him, was a great compliment. For two years, Maury guided Thomas's study of Latin, Greek, classical literature, mathematics, and other subjects. The boy valued Maury's mastery of Greek and Latin, but disliked his tutor's narrow views. Maury denounced anyone who did not belong to the Church of England, and he eventually took Britain's side in its disputes with the American colonies.

In 1760, when he was 17, Jefferson decided that he had learned all that he could from Maury. He therefore wrote a letter to John Harvie, one of his guardians, asking permission to attend the College of William and Mary at Williamsburg, the capital of Virginia. Harvie found this idea sensible, and soon Jefferson traveled, with his slave Jupiter, to Williamsburg, the first town of any size that he had seen. In the 1770s, Williamsburg had about 2,000 inhabitants, nearly half of them African slaves. The town was a collection of modest, well-tended brick and wooden buildings. At its center were the capitol, the governor's palace, and the College of William and Mary.

"IT WOULD BE TO MY ADVANTAGE TO GO TO THE COLLEGE"

Writing on January 14, 1760, the 16-year-old Thomas Jefferson sought to persuade his guardian, John Harvie, to allow him to attend the College of William and Mary, in Williamsburg, Virginia. Harvie granted permission, and the young Jefferson became an eager and brilliant student at William and Mary. His experience there, however, left him dissatisfied with the education offered by Virginia's only college and with the architecture of the college buildings. This is the earliest letter from his pen that survives.

Sir,—I was at Colo. Peter Randolph's about a Fortnight ago, & my Schooling falling into Discourse, he said he thought it would be to my Advantage to go to the College, & was desirous I should go, as indeed I am myself for several Reasons. In the first place as long as I stay at the Mountains the Loss of one fourth of my Time is inevitable, by Company's coming here & detaining me from School. And likewise my Absence will in great Measure put a Stop to so much Company, & by that Means lessen the Expences of the Estate in House-Keeping. And on the other Hand by going to the College I shall get a more universal Acquaintance, which may hereafter be serviceable to me, & I suppose I can pursue my Studies in the Greek & Latin as well there as here, & likewise learn something of the Mathematics. I shall be glad of your opinion.

William and Mary was the second-oldest college in America (after Harvard). By modern standards, it was not much of a college. Most students paid little attention to academic requirements or to learning. Nearly all of the courses were lectures; professors seemed not to care whether their students showed up. Like their counterparts at the English universities of Oxford and Cambridge, students at William and Mary devoted their energy and enthusiasm to betting on horse races, playing dice and cards, and courting ladies. Though Jefferson sampled these distractions, he preferred to throw himself into study. His main diversion was his enthusiasm for his violin. Indeed, during the Christmas holidays just before he entered William and Mary, he met another young violinist, Patrick Henry; the two musicians entertained their fellow holiday revelers during the two-week vacation.

Jefferson attended William and Mary from 1760 until his graduation in 1762. His true education took place outside the classroom, thanks to Professor William Small. Small, who taught mathematics and "natural philosophy" (what we call science), was the college's best professor, and the only one who was not a minister of the Church of England. Barely 10 years older than Jefferson, Small befriended the gangly, redheaded student and introduced him to Francis Fauquier, Virginia's lieutenant governor, and George Wythe, a prominent lawyer.

Jefferson soon became a regular member of this cheerful, learned group, who treated him as a younger equal. Jefferson drank in all that he could learn from them, and Fauquier often assembled Jefferson and other musicians to join him in informal concerts of chamber music. The greatest legacy of Jefferson's college years was his friendship with Wythe. Born in 1725, Wythe was one of the two leading attorneys in Virginia and was famous for his learning and culture. He often discussed law with Jefferson, who decided to study law with Wythe after his graduation from William and Mary.

In this period, there were no law schools. Instead, a would-be lawyer "read law" under the guidance of an established

member of the bar. Reading law meant two things: studying (and puzzling over) legal treatises; and the drudgery of copying writs (the legal documents used to conduct lawsuits), wills, contracts, and letters. Copying was supposed to pound into the student's brain the form of legal documents and the feel of legal language.

The law books that most English and American lawyers studied were the works of the 17th-century jurist Sir Edward Coke. Coke's writings boiled down the wisdom of English law as established by decades of judicial decisions and elaborated by generations of lawyers—a system known as "common law." Coke wrote in the convoluted, thorny prose of the 17th century, and on Christmas Day of 1762 the young Jefferson complained bitterly in a letter to his friend John Page, "I do wish the Devil had old Coke, for I am sure I never was so tired of an old dull scoundrel in my life." It was a view he shared with nearly every law student of his time, but, unlike most of them, Jefferson learned his Coke thoroughly.

Wythe was not just a lawyer but a scholar, and he refused to let Jefferson's legal training rest on the threadbare formula of Coke and copying. Rather, he used a plan modeled on his own habits of thought and reading; he wanted his students to love the law as a body of learning, to be devoted to its study, and to adopt high standards of legal research and argument. Wythe had Jefferson read history, philosophy, and ethics to provide intellectual context for the dry materials of the law. When Jefferson later trained aspiring lawyers, he used the plan of legal education that Wythe had used with him.

Wythe instructed three generations of Virginia lawyers, but Jefferson was his favorite student, and Jefferson revered his mentor. Jefferson even modeled his small, neat handwriting and his rejection of capital letters to begin sentences on Wythe's. The two remained friends and political allies until Wythe's tragic murder by poisoning in 1806, apparently the deed of a grandson angered by Wythe's decision to cut him out of his will. On August 31, 1820, Jefferson sketched Wythe's life for the biographer John Sanderson, painting Wythe as more virtuous than the Roman senator Marcus Cato, a role model for 18th-century Americans steeped in Greek and Roman classics:

> No man left behind him a character more venerated.... His virtue was of the purest tint, and, devoted as he was to liberty, and the natural and equal rights of men, he might truly be called the Cato of his country, without the avarice of the Roman; for a more disinterested person never lived. Temperance and regularity in all his habits gave him general good health, and his unaffected modesty and suavity of manner endeared him to every one.... Such was George Wythe, the honor of his own, and model of future times.

In 1767, after studying with Wythe for nearly five years (more than twice as long as the usual course of reading law), Jefferson became a member of the Virginia bar. He did not have to face the bar exam that modern lawyers must pass. Rather, Wythe swore to a committee of established lawyers that his student was honorable, able, and well trained. Then Jefferson answered the lawyers' questions on legal issues. Finally, he took the oath of membership and dined with his sponsor and examiners.

Jefferson lived up to Wythe's hopes for him. His learning, his literary and legal talent, and his membership in two of

Virginia's great families vaulted him into the top rank of Virginia's lawyers. Like Wythe, he established a legal practice that focused on issues of real property and inheritance; in colonial Virginia such matters were of vital interest to the planters who gave lawyers most of their business. Also like Wythe, he was more attracted to the intellectual side of lawyering than to the work of the courtroom, but he tried his share of cases and won many of them.

In November 1774, Jefferson retired from practicing law. He and his colleagues had protested the low legal fees mandated by Virginia's laws, but he had another reason for giving up the practice of law: he did not need to support himself that way. He saw himself first as a gentleman planter. A farmer tilled the soil with his own hands, whereas a planter hired help (or bought slaves) to run his farm for him. A gentleman was a man who was independent—that is, his source of income did not depend on an employer. Gentlemen were not expected to worry about making ends meet; they were supposedly above such matters. Also, gentlemen were supposed to behave in ways that suited members

In this house in Williamsburg, Virginia, George Wythe trained three generations of lawyers, including John Marshall and Henry Clay, but Thomas Jefferson was his favorite student.

of the social and political elite. They were expected to govern themselves, to be careful about how they spoke and acted. In particular, they sought to safeguard their honor and reputation, for these made a gentleman's word worth taking, entitled him to the respect of his neighbors and his social inferiors, and made him trustworthy in business and worthy of political leadership.

By birth and training, Jefferson was a young gentleman of Virginia, a member in good standing of the province's governing class. Thus, it was no surprise when in 1768 his neighbors elected Jefferson to represent them in the House of Burgesses, the Virginia legislature's lower house. He did not have to campaign for office. Instead, his election was a matter of ceremony. Voters, guided by the community's leading gentlemen, agreed to elect the candidate pre-chosen by that group. A candidate would treat the voters to drinks, either by rolling large barrels of punch and hard cider onto his lawn or by throwing a party at a convenient tavern. When two leading men wanted the same office, they competed for their neighbors' votes by handing out food and drink. On election day, each voter would step up to the ballot box and announce his choice, receiving the candidate's thanks and enduring the jeers of those on the other side.

Jefferson seemed to be a typical member of the planter elite. However, his surviving papers show that he was different. He was more interested in the life of the mind, more intellectually venturesome, more inclined to question established customs. Like other educated gentlemen of his time, he kept a notebook into which he copied extracts from books that struck his fancy. The author to whom he devoted the most space in his notebook was the controversial skeptic Lord Bolingbroke, whose questioning of Christianity and opposition to political corruption struck chords with Jefferson.

In August 1771, Jefferson gave Robert Skipwith (one of his in-laws) a list of books that should be included in a gentleman's library—a list that offers clues as to his own reading. He recommended key authors of the Enlightenment, such as Locke, Hume, Bolingbroke, and Montesquieu, and advocated the habits of wide and deep reading that Wythe had taught him. He kept his daring speculations on religion to himself, however. Few of his contemporaries knew what was lurking in his mind and heart.

At this time, Jefferson prepared to set up an independent home for himself. As Peter Jefferson's oldest son, he had inherited most of his father's estate, including his birthplace, Shadwell, where he lived with his mother and sisters. Jefferson never explained his reasons for moving, but we know, for one thing, that he was doing what other planters did. Many planters built several houses, each the nerve center of its own plantation; if they had to sell a plantation, it would sell more easily with a ready-to-occupy house. Further, he may have wanted to try out his budding architectural ideas, inspired by studying the works of the 16th-century Italian architect Andrea Palladio.

Jefferson chose for his building site a low hill four miles from Shadwell; he leveled the hilltop and began to plan a house that he called Monticello, from the Italian word for "little hill." In February 1770, a fire at Shadwell, which destroyed his first library and his painstakingly amassed collection of legal notes and papers, spurred his plans. Monticello became one of the chief joys of his life, blending hobby and obsession.

Jefferson also may have begun Monticello as a home for a future wife. Young, wealthy, handsome, and of good family, he was a highly eligible bachelor. In Virginia, as in England, single gentlemen and ladies sought one another out in an elaborate, formal process of courtship. A key goal of this process was to improve their social and economic standing by uniting their fortunes and estates. Jefferson was aware of this principle, but he also held highly romantic views of women. As a college student, he courted the local beauty Rebecca Burwell, but she rejected him, later marrying his friend Jacquelin Ambler. He brooded over this rejection in letters to his friends that mingled heavy-handed humor with great helpings of self-pity, and he consoled himself with his violin. In the late 1760s, after his admission to the bar, he befriended a neighboring planter, John Walker. Unfortunately, he also developed a strong passion for Walker's wife; he tried, as he later admitted, to seduce her, but she spurned his advances. (His clumsy gallantry came back to haunt him four decades later.)

Finally, he found someone who suited him and whom he suited—Martha Wayles Skelton, a recent widow and one of Virginia's wealthiest women. They married on January 1, 1772, in a wedding hosted by her father, the planter, lawyer, and slave trader John Wayles. Thomas was 28 and Martha was 23. Two weeks later, braving snowdrifts and treacherous roads, the newlyweds arrived at Monticello, which was just a building site with only one habitable room, what is now Monticello's South Pavilion.

No portrait of Martha Jefferson survives, but we know that she was short, slight, and famed for her beauty and talents. Like Jefferson, she loved music. As the story goes, when other suitors found her playing a duet on her harpsichord with Jefferson on his violin, they decided that he had won the day. She was an able household manager, she shared some of Jefferson's tastes in reading (they both loved Laurence Sterne's comic novel *Tristram Shandy*), and she did not favor his political career, preferring him to remain home.

By 1772, when Jefferson married, his way of life was under siege. Most Virginia planters raised tobacco, but the crop was hard to grow and leached nutrients out of the soil at an alarming rate. Battling the problem of exhausted farmland, planters rotated crops from plantation to plantation, letting the worn-out soil renew itself. Thus, prominent planters owned several plantations, having bought them, inherited them, or acquired them through marriage. The need for good land drove them to look westward, to expand their holdings or to speculate in buying and selling land.

Virginia planters and farmers faced a more ominous burden—debt. Farming has always been a hard way to make a living. Virginia planters and farmers not only had to borrow money to buy land and seed to grow the crops on which they depended; they also had to hire overseers and buy slaves. Though they did not pay the slaves, they had to feed, house, and clothe them. Great planters found farming as hard and risky as small farmers. They kept watch over the weather, the soil's condition, and the prices their crops fetched at market. They dreaded downturns in prices, which would reduce the money they could use to pay their debts.

Obsessed with debt, Virginia planters and farmers kept careful account books, listing every debt they owed and every debt owed to them. Such "book debts" often took the place of cash. For example, a planter would give a note (a written promise to pay) in exchange for goods he wanted to buy. A note set forth the amount he owed, the rate of interest he would have to pay, the date when he assumed the debt, and the date when it would come due. The person receiving the note would record it in his account books so that he, or his heirs, would know what he was owed and be able to collect when the time was right. Sometimes one planter would take a debt owed to him by a second and sign it over as payment for a debt he owed to a third, or to a merchant. Such transactions became tangled over the years.

Complex networks of debt linked colonial planters to one another and to merchants in Williamsburg, Baltimore, Philadelphia, and London. Although planters kept track of debts owed to them and debts they owed, they still amassed debts. Being a planter meant keeping up appearances—in particular, giving the impression of carefree wealth. Thus, planters would give dinners for two or three dozen guests with many courses and fine wines; they would put up visitors for days or weeks at a time; and they would purchase from Europe the best clothing, furniture, hunting dogs, and firearms. For example, the newlywed Jefferson ordered his

London agent to buy the finest new pianoforte for Martha, and he regularly made other luxury purchases—fabrics, books, wines, sheet music and musical instruments, furniture, even carriages—all on credit, each bringing another debt.

Virginia's planters, entangled in debt, often likened themselves to flies caught in a spider's web, even though these webs were mostly of their own making. They thought that, because they were gentlemen, their mere word was guarantee enough that they would repay their debts. They resented merchants' and moneylenders' demands for payment, for those demands implied that they could not be trusted to repay.

Jefferson was a typical man of his time and social standing. Once he became an adult, he began the luxurious way of life that he followed until his death, piling up debts in the process. In 1773, John Wayles, his father-in-law, died, leaving vast landholdings to his daughter Martha, which, under Virginia law, actually went to Jefferson as her husband. Because Wayles owned many slaves, this inheritance made Jefferson one of the largest slaveholders in Virginia. (One of these slaves was Betty Hemings, with whom Wayles had had a sexual relationship that produced at least one daughter, Sally Hemings; Martha Wayles Jefferson and Sally Hemings were half-sisters.) However, Wayles had used many of his

RUN away from the subscriber in *Albemarle*, a Mulatto slave called *Sandy*, about 35 years of age, his stature is rather low, inclining to corpulence, and his complexion light; he is a shoemaker by trade, in which he uses his left hand principally, can do coarse carpenters work, and is something of a horse jockey; he is greatly addicted to drink, and when drunk is insolent and disorderly, in his conversation he swears much, and in his behaviour is artful and knavish. He took with him a white horse, much scarred with traces, of which it is expected he will endeavour to dispose; he also carried his shoemakers tools, and will probably endeavour to get employment that way. Whoever conveys the said slave to me, in *Albemarle*, shall have 40 s. reward, if taken up within the county, 4 l. if elsewhere within the colony, and 10 l. if in any other colony. from
THOMAS JEFFERSON.

On September 14, 1769, Thomas Jefferson placed this advertisement in the Virginia Gazette seeking aid in recovering a runaway slave named Sandy. As was usual in such ads, Jefferson gave a detailed word-portrait of Sandy's appearance, habits, abilities, and distinguishing traits.

lands to guarantee his debts. When he borrowed money, he used land to secure the loan, so that the lender either would be repaid or could take the pledged land for himself.

Jefferson faced a problem, one that also faced his fellow heirs. Should they pay the estate's debts first, and take what was left? Or should they take the lands, and their accompanying burden of debt, in the hope that they could farm them or sell them and make enough money to pay those debts? In the end, they split the difference, selling some lands but keeping others.

The problem was that, by taking the lands with the debts, the heirs put their entire fortunes under the shadow of the debts that John Wayles owed at his death. These transactions transformed the nature of the debts. Before, they were attached to the land, like a mortgage. After, they became personal obligations of the person who took possession of the land, and all of that person's assets would be at risk when the time came to satisfy the debt.

As a lawyer, Jefferson should have known that he was putting his financial future at risk, but, as he so often did, he hoped that he would find a way to pay off these debts and trusted the future. Unfortunately, the future dashed his hopes. This was the first of a series of transactions by which he saddled himself with ever-growing debts that haunted him until his own death more than half a century later.

Even in normal times, the problem of debt loomed large for the Virginia elite, embittering their relations with British creditors. However, in the 1760s and 1770s, growing disputes between the colonies and Britain disrupted the network of debts linking Virginia to London. These developments set in motion political, legal, social, and economic forces that would lift Jefferson to great historical importance and, at the same time, mount new assaults on the social and economic leadership of Jefferson and those like him.

"WE HOLD THESE TRUTHS..." (1763–1776)

In 1763, the 20-year-old Thomas Jefferson was a proud subject of King George III who never dreamed that, by the time he was 33, he would help to break up Britain's American empire. The American Revolution transformed Jefferson. Not only did it give him a focus and sense of mission—a chance to be not just a politician but a statesman—it also inspired his first creative political and intellectual labors, and gave him his greatest claims to fame.

When Jefferson was elected to the Virginia House of Burgesses in 1768, he joined radical members such as Patrick Henry and George Washington against those backing the royal governor. Virginia's politics were like politics in the other colonies. Although each colony had unique issues, their politics all followed a general pattern, pitting officials sent from England to govern the colonies (and their local allies) against those colonists who sought to govern themselves.

Gentlemen planters made up Virginia's governing class. Understanding their political role as one of leadership by right of birth, they saw legislative seats as their personal property. Sometimes, someone not born into that class might win power. For example, Patrick Henry used his speech-making gifts to build his legal career and to win a seat in the House of Burgesses. Henry's great talent was swaying juries; he had tried to study law with George Wythe, but scorned reading and research as drudgery. Jefferson admired Henry's oratory, but he looked down on him, too. As he reminisced for the biographer William Wirt in 1812, "In ordinary business he was a very inefficient member. He could not draw a bill on the most simple subject which would bear legal criticism, or even the ordinary criticism which looks to correctness of style & ideas, for indeed there was no accuracy of idea in his head."

Fortunately for Jefferson, one did not have to be an orator to win the respect of the House of Burgesses. All his life he disliked public speaking; his voice was not suited to the task, and his shyness before a large gathering made any speech an ordeal. Instead, he earned his colleagues' esteem with his capacity for hard work, his tact, his mastery of parliamentary procedure, and his talent with his pen. Jefferson was especially good at drafting legislation and resolutions; he could distill the sense of a legislative gathering into vigorous, elegant prose.

Jefferson's literary ability won him an important role in the years-old but growing conflict between the colonies and Great Britain. In 1763, at the end of the Seven Years' War (known in America as the French and Indian War), George III had no subjects more loyal than those in the 13 colonies of British North America. Boasting that they were subjects of the freest empire on earth, Americans took the phrase "I am a freeborn Englishman" as a badge of honor. (Most of them ignored the irony that freeborn Englishmen regularly owned or dealt in slaves.)

After 1763, a fiscal crisis posed the first threat to the Empire's internal peace. Victory in the wars against France had been expensive; Britain had piled up staggering debts, and the British people grumbled at the taxes levied to pay those debts. Because these wars had been fought mostly to protect Britain's colonial empire, Parliament reasoned, those who benefited from that protection ought to shoulder some of the burden of paying for it. Thus, Parliament began to impose taxes on the Americans. In 1765, Parliament enacted and George III approved the first such tax, the Stamp Act, on printed and paper goods. Payment was symbolized by a stamp that had to be affixed to contracts, newspapers, court documents, even decks of cards. The revenue raised by the Stamp Act would help reduce Britain's war debts, or so Parliament and the king hoped.

The Stamp Act imposed on the colonies a tax identical to one levied in Britain, but many colonists hated it, and not just because they did not want to pay taxes. They saw the issue as one of principle. Because no colonist could vote for a member of the House of Commons, the colonists argued, Parliament could not enact any tax to raise revenue from the colonies. Only the colonial legislatures, where the Americans were represented, could do that. Many colonists admitted that Britain had the power to regulate trade between its colonies and Europe, a power that included the power to impose taxes to help regulate trade. But they insisted that Parliament could not raise money by taxing people who were not in fact represented in Parliament. They maintained that those taxes violated their English constitutional right to be taxed only by legislatures that they actually elected themselves. This argument was the basis of the slogan "No taxation without representation."

British politicians and writers embraced a theory of representation at odds with the colonists' view. They argued that all British subjects, wherever they lived in the Empire, were represented in Parliament, whether they voted for members of the House of Commons or not. The reason was that members of Parliament had to represent the interests not just of their own constituents, but of the whole Empire. This doctrine of virtual representation made actual representation, which the Americans demanded, unnecessary.

The dispute with Britain became more than a dispute about representation. Protests against the Stamp Act rocked the colonies. Rioters beat and harassed stamp agents and burned the hated stamps. In a fiery speech to the Virginia House of Burgesses, Patrick Henry declared, "Caesar had his Brutus, Charles the first, his Cromwell, and George the third may profit by their example. . . ." The young Jefferson, standing in the foyer and listening, was dazzled by Henry's speech; as he recalled in his autobiography, "Mr. Henry's talents as a popular orator. . . were great indeed, such as I have never heard from any other man. He appeared to me to speak as Homer wrote."

As discontent spread through British North America, politicians in each colony began to reach across colonial borders. In October 1765, in the first intercolonial meeting, delegates from all the American colonies except Georgia met in New York City to coordinate American resistance to British policies. This Stamp Act Congress adopted a set of defiant resolutions and endorsed a boycott of British goods.

The British government could ignore the resolutions, but British merchants desperate for American trade could not ignore the boycott. In 1766, Parliament repealed the Stamp Act. At the same time, however, it enacted the Declaratory Act, which announced that Parliament had the right to make laws for the colonies "in all cases whatsoever." The colonists soon learned what Parliament had in mind. In the late 1760s, Parliament enacted more taxes, keeping the issue of taxation alive. Colonial merchants tried to avoid the taxes by smuggling goods past customs officials, launching a grim battle of wits with British authorities. Meanwhile, astute lawyers and politicians such as Jefferson kept careful track of the arguments and controversies generated between the mother country and her colonies.

The sharpest conflicts unfolded in Boston, the capital of Massachusetts and, after Philadelphia, the second-largest city in British North America. Impatient with the riots that broke out in Boston's streets, and with the smuggling that spurred the city's prosperity, the king's ministers sent British regiments (nicknamed "redcoats" or "lobsterbacks") to Boston to keep the peace—though using a standing army to police civilians violated principles of English liberty as the Americans understood them.

Many colonists outside New England grumbled at the brawls between Britain and Massachusetts. Boston's fight, some said, was not Pennsylvania's fight, or New York's, or North Carolina's. Most colonists felt stronger ties to the mother country than to neighboring colonies; the 13 colonies varied widely in economy, religion, even dialect and accent, and they looked on one another with suspicion and distrust.

Jefferson, by contrast, saw that Americans had common interests at least as important as their differences. He insisted that the colonists all were freeborn Englishmen, with the same rights as anyone born in Great Britain. His radicalism was the other side of the coin of his pride in being a British subject. He thought that a Virginia gentleman was as good as—and entitled to the same rights as—any native-born Englishman. Jefferson thus became an early backer of the American cause, watching with wary concern as relations between Boston and London worsened.

In the spring of 1773, Jefferson and other members of Virginia's House of Burgesses devised a plan to cement ties among the American colonies. They proposed the founding of a "committee of correspondence," a group of politicians who would write letters to like-minded politicians in other colonies to share ideas, spread news, and coordinate strategy and tactics for resisting British colonial policies. Richard Henry Lee hit on the idea, and Jefferson penned the resolution. Jefferson's boyhood friend, Dabney Carr, made the speech proposing the resolution to the legislature, which passed it after brisk debate. Carr, Lee, and Jefferson were among the ten men named to the committee.

The alliance between Carr and Jefferson had deep roots, for the two men had been close friends since childhood, and Carr had married Jefferson's beloved sister Martha.

Their political and personal partnership seemed destined for great things, but on May 16, 1773, Carr died of a sudden fever, five months before his 30th birthday. When they were schoolboys, Carr and Jefferson had studied together under a large oak on the grounds of what became Monticello; they had agreed that the first to die should be buried under that tree. The grieving Jefferson buried Carr there; that grave was the first in the cemetery that he laid out for himself and his family. Ever afterward, Jefferson insisted that Carr had been far more talented than he was, and that Carr's death was a calamity for Virginia and for America.

Jefferson had to put aside his mourning for his friend and carry on their efforts in defense of American liberty. In 1773, the king's ministers hit on a plan that, they hoped, would accomplish three linked goals. It would ease colonists' resentment of their tax burdens, help the powerful but financially ailing East India Company (which controlled trade with British colonies in India, and in which many British leaders had large investments), and boost tax revenues from America. First, Parliament repealed all taxes on America except the three-penny tax on tea. Then British officials worked with the East India Company to get rid of its huge surplus of Indian tea.

That fall, fleets of ships sailed to North American ports, their holds crammed with surplus tea priced at bargain rates. British officials reasoned that the tea was priced so low, even with the tax, that colonists would buy it all. The resulting revenue would be a windfall for the government, and the East India Company would be rid of its surplus. They were wrong on all counts.

When the tea ships reached America, some ports let the ships dock but refused to receive the tea; others turned the ships away. The captains of the three ships sent to Boston decided that they had no choice but to dock and wait; nervous customs officials were not sure what to do. Bostonians took the decision out of their hands.

On the night of December 16, 1773, members of the Sons of Liberty, the resistance organization led by such men as Samuel Adams, disguised themselves as Indian warriors and headed for Boston Harbor. They stormed the tea ships and threw 342 chests of the hated tea overboard. One raider, a locksmith, broke open the ships' holds and afterward repaired each lock, to demonstrate that this "mob" respected property rights and objected only to the illegitimate tax on tea. When the raiders discovered that one of the group had stuffed his pockets with tea for his own use, they dumped the tea into the water, stripped him naked, and made him walk home that way, in the freezing cold.

When news of this "Boston Tea Party" reached London in early 1774, Parliament and the king, outraged by what they saw as a mob's destruction of property, enacted a series

Paul Revere's engraving of the Boston Massacre presented the colonists' view of British soldiers as bloodthirsty and cruel. The Massacre outraged Jefferson and other Americans far beyond Massachusetts.

of statutes to punish Boston and Massachusetts. They revoked the colony's charter, the document granted by the Crown that authorized the colony's government, and imposed a military government on Massachusetts. They also closed the port of Boston to trade until Bostonians repaid the full value of the tea that had been dumped into the harbor.

Charging that these "Intolerable Acts" denied the people of Massachusetts the rights of Englishmen, many colonists realized that what had happened to Massachusetts could happen to New York, Georgia, or Virginia. Leading American politicians agreed that the colonists had to develop a strategy of resistance to these tyrannical measures.

Virginia took the lead in organizing resistance, and Jefferson played a key role in this campaign. The House of Burgesses drafted resolutions denouncing the Intolerable Acts, but the royal governor, Lord Dunmore, would not stand for those measures. In response, Jefferson and his colleagues hit upon a brilliant maneuver. They drafted a resolution proposing a day of fasting and prayer in support of Massachusetts; then they persuaded one of their most respectable conservative colleagues, Robert Carter Nicholas, to offer the measure, which easily passed.

As Jefferson recalled, the day of fasting and prayer strengthened Virginians' fellowship with the people of Massachusetts and their commitment to the American cause. Infuriated, Governor Dunmore dissolved Virginia's General Assembly. The burgesses walked down Williamsburg's main street, Duke of Gloucester Street, from the Capitol to the Apollo Tavern, where they adopted a resolution calling for a continental congress, a gathering of delegates from all the colonies to coordinate resistance to Britain's actions. The meeting place would be Philadelphia, the largest city in British North America and a central location convenient to delegates from all the colonies. No such body had met since the Stamp Act Congress of 1765, nine years before.

Jefferson drafted a set of instructions to guide Virginia's delegates, but some of his colleagues thought that it sounded too radical and refused to adopt it. Impressed by his draft's eloquence and power, his friends published it as a pamphlet, and it was reprinted in London. "A Summary View of the Rights of British America," Jefferson's first major political work, showed his mastery of the constitutional dispute between Britain and the colonists, his commitment to the American position, and his masterly style.

Jefferson argued that the colonists were entitled to the rights of British subjects because they and their ancestors chose to settle in America, founding and building the colonies unaided by the mother country. Thus, he insisted, they and their descendants had all the rights of freeborn Englishmen. (By contrast, British authorities claimed that England had conquered North America. Under the unwritten English constitution, conquest meant that inhabitants of conquered territories could have only those rights that the conquering power chose to recognize.) All Englishmen had the right to be taxed only by a legislature in which they were represented directly. Parliament could only make laws for and levy taxes on Great Britain. Because each colony had a legislature that could make laws and levy taxes, Parliament had no right to legislate for America. In fact, Jefferson concluded, the only thing that Americans had in common with those residing in Britain was loyalty to King George III.

The "Summary View" made another argument for the colonists' rights, based on Jefferson's idealized view of English history. As he saw it, the ancient Anglo-Saxons had governed themselves under unchanging principles of liberty. Although in 1066 the Normans conquered England, they learned to govern by these principles. Jefferson argued that, because the colonists were true to these timeless principles, they were the true heirs of the Anglo-Saxon heritage of constitutional liberty. He charged further that Britain's attempts to limit the colonists' liberties were therefore tyrannical and unjust.

Jefferson concluded his pamphlet with a moving challenge to the king to live up to his constitutional responsibilities:

> [Americans] know, and will therefore say, that kings are the servants, not the proprietors of the people. Open your breast, sire, to liberal and expanded thought. Let not the name of George the third be a blot in the page of history. You are surrounded by British counsellors, but remember that they are parties. You have no ministers for American affairs, because you have none taken from among us....It behoves you, therefore, to think and to act for yourself and your people. The great principles of right and wrong are legible to every reader; to pursue them requires not the aid of many counsellors. The whole art of government consists in the art of being honest. Only aim to do your duty, and mankind will give you credit where you fail.

The "Summary View" won Jefferson admirers among American and British opponents of the government's policy, and bolstered his stature as an advocate of the American cause. In Britain, however, his lecture to George III left lasting bitterness in the king's heart, and the king's ministers set Jefferson down as an enemy.

Meeting in the fall of 1774, the First Continental Congress adopted a set of resolutions restating the Americans' arguments against Britain. More important, it launched a boycott of British goods. Throughout the colonies, committees pledged to abide by and to enforce this new boycott, known as the Association; these actions drew the colonists together in resistance and began to sap trade with Britain.

The success of the First Continental Congress spurred its delegates to plan a second, to meet in May of 1775. Events outpaced their expectations. On April 19, 1775, four weeks before the Second Continental Congress was to gather in Philadelphia, British soldiers and Massachusetts militiamen fought a skirmish at Lexington, followed by the battle of Concord. The British retreat from Concord to Boston was a running battle, sharp and bloody, with infuriated militiamen picking off soldiers and officers along the way. The dispute between Britain and America had turned from a war of words and arguments into a military struggle.

Shocked by the bloodshed in Massachusetts, the Second Continental Congress created the Continental Army and named Virginia delegate George Washington its commander in chief. As Washington took command of the forces camped outside Boston, Congress and the colonists were unsure what to do next. For the first time, the question of independence was at issue.

Some delegates—chiefly New Englanders, but backed by Virginians such as Washington, Jefferson, Patrick Henry, and Richard Henry Lee—insisted that Britain's use of force had severed the ties between the mother country and her colonies. Americans, they insisted, should embrace independence and fight to achieve it. Others—mostly from New York, Pennsylvania, and the Carolinas—insisted that the Continental Army should wage war only to defend the colonists' English liberties. That resistance would shatter the arrogance of Parliament and the king's ministers, and would persuade George III to mediate the dispute. They argued that any attempt to win independence would be a disaster for America and for the British Empire.

Why was independence controversial? Ever since the first rumblings of discontent with British rule in 1765, the colonists had insisted—as Jefferson maintained in the "Summary View"—that they were not interested in independence, but were loyal British subjects defending true principles of English liberty. Not only would declaring independence be treason, a crime that carried the death penalty, it also meant that Americans would be giving up their cherished status as freeborn Englishmen, which they did not want to do. Besides, not since the days of ancient Greece had a colony succeeded in a war for independence. Parliament and the king's ministers refused to believe, however, that the colonists wanted to remain within the Empire. Instead, British officials insisted that a conspiracy of evil-minded, treasonous politicians were fomenting resistance, and seeking independence, solely to advance themselves.

At its core, this argument was a dispute about the nature and principles of the unwritten English constitution—and there was no constitutional way out. Each side championed a competing interpretation of that constitution. Both versions were rooted in the constitutional, political, and military struggles that tore England apart in the 17th century.

The British claimed that Parliament was supreme within the English system, because Parliament had won that role as part of the 1689 settlement enshrining its victory over the tyranny of the Stuart kings Charles I and James II. By contrast, the Americans claimed that no institution in the English system was supreme. Rather, to protect the rights of all Englishmen, the English constitution imposed a system of limits on "arbitrary" (unchecked) power. That system balanced the king and the two houses of Parliament (the House of Commons and the House of Lords), restraining all three institutions so that no one of them could violate the liberties of British subjects. The question of where Americans would fit in that system never received a clear answer.

Americans on all sides hoped that George III would act as an impartial "patriot king," mediating the dispute between Parliament and the Americans in the interests of all his subjects. Indeed, Jefferson had closed his "Summary View" with such an appeal. On July 5, 1775, the Second Continental Congress sent the king a last petition, signed by all the delegates, including Jefferson, begging him to intervene between Parliament and America. But George III rejected the Americans' view of the controversy.

By the summer of 1775 the king's patience had run out. Not only did he refuse to receive their "Olive Branch Petition," on August 23, 1775, he issued a proclamation denouncing the "traitorous correspondence, counsels and comfort of diverse wicked and desperate persons within this realm" and ordered "all our Officers, as well civil as military, and all others our obedient and loyal subjects, to use their utmost endeavors to withstand and suppress such rebellion, and to disclose and make known all treasons and traitorous conspiracies which they shall know to be against us, our crown and dignity...."

George III might have hoped that his proclamation and his soldiers would frighten the colonists out of rebelliousness, but his actions backfired. First, he infuriated many Americans, who no longer thought of him as the good king they had revered. Next, he proved that there was no generally accepted umpire within the English constitutional system who could work out a compromise agreeable to the mother country and the colonists. Thus, the king's words and deeds made him the focus of American resentment and pushed Americans further along a path that most had not wanted to tread—that of independence.

When he was a delegate to the Second Continental Congress, Jefferson rented rooms in this Philadelphia boardinghouse. Here he prepared the first draft of the Declaration of Independence. Jefferson later declared that his goal in writing the Declaration was to express "the American mind."

That fall, more and more colonists came to realize that, if they wished to remain loyal to George III, they could not stay in the land of their birth. One of these was John Randolph, an older cousin of Jefferson who had become the king's Attorney General in Virginia. In 1771, Randolph and Jefferson had made a friendly agreement, drafted by Patrick Henry and witnessed by seven friends (including Wythe and Henry), having to do with a violin owned by Randolph that Jefferson coveted. The agreement was that, if Randolph died before Jefferson, his estate would deliver Randolph's violin and sheet music to Jefferson; if Jefferson died before Randolph, his estate would deliver to Randolph his choice of books to the value of 100 pounds.

Now Randolph's decision to leave for England meant that he needed money; he let Jefferson know that he was willing to sell his violin. Jefferson paid Randolph 13 pounds for it, and he played it until he broke his wrist in an accident in 1786. Jefferson and Randolph continued to correspond after Randolph arrived in England, but their parting—and the fate of their bet over Randolph's violin—reflected the larger, growing rift between Britain and America.

By January 1776, Americans were ready to be persuaded that independence was legitimate and desirable. The pamphlet *Common Sense,* published that month, supplied that persuasion. Written by the journalist Thomas Paine, *Common Sense* presented a powerful case for independence. Attacking George III in particular and kingship in general, Paine insisted that monarchy was illegitimate, and that no monarch could have any claim on the loyalty or allegiance of a free people; this argument helped to cut the last tie binding many Americans to Britain. He further argued that America had the right to embrace independence and the ability and resources to make it a reality, answering the fears that many Americans still had about the risks of declaring independence.

In the spring of 1776, as British forces and the Continental Army prepared to do battle in New York, Americans were on the edge of claiming independence. Royal officials fled, and self-appointed provincial congresses and conventions took over the tasks of government and adopted resolutions rejecting British authority, demanding independence, or both. At the same time, these bodies, aware that their constituents wanted legitimate government, begged the Second Continental Congress for instructions and guidance. On May 15, 1776, after months of debate, Congress adopted a resolution (written by John Adams of Massachusetts) calling on the colonies to frame new forms of government, blaming the necessity of this step on George III. Congress began to keep pace with the quickening currents of public opinion. It was only a matter of time before they would have to face the issue of independence directly.

Jefferson had kept careful watch over the unfolding crisis from Virginia, but he almost missed his chance to serve in Congress, because he had to deal with his mother's sudden death and the Virginia convention's difficulties in shoring up the provincial government after Lord Dunmore fled. He made up for lost time once he arrived in Philadelphia.

The new delegate befriended Benjamin Franklin and John Adams. Franklin was the most celebrated American in the world. His achievements as a printer, writer, scientist, inventor, politician, and philanthropist spanned the range of human pursuits. In 1775, at the age of 69, after nearly two decades as an American lobbyist in London, he had returned to Philadelphia to take a seat in the Second Continental Congress. Some Americans suspected that his years abroad made him too sympathetic to Britain. They were wrong.

Franklin had grown disgusted with British shortsightedness and snobbery and seethed with rage because His Majesty's Government had publicly humiliated him. Thus, Franklin returned to America as a committed member of Congress's radical bloc. Because Franklin and Jefferson saw eye to eye on politics and shared an interest in subjects such as science, they soon became mutual admirers. All his life,

Jefferson venerated Franklin and carefully recorded anecdotes showcasing the older man's wit, wisdom, and geniality.

Jefferson's relationship with John Adams was more complex, for they were nearly opposite in every way. Eight years older than Jefferson, the outspoken Adams was one of Congress's most controversial delegates; the tactful Jefferson easily won his peers' respect. Adams was what we would call a middle-class New Englander; Jefferson was a Virginia aristocrat. Adams was of average height and stout; Jefferson was tall and thin. Adams was a powerful, effective orator; Jefferson hated public speaking and was notably bad at it. Though they were two of the finest lawyers of their era, Adams was as skilled a courtroom pleader as he was a legal scholar, whereas Jefferson preferred the quiet of the study to the tumult of the trial. Adams's character was steeped in his ancestors' Puritan values; Jefferson was more inclined to the pursuits of this world than the next. Painfully self-critical and introspective, Adams had the valuable gift of being able to laugh at himself and the world around him; Jefferson, more polished and affable, lacked humor and tended not to doubt himself. Despite, or perhaps because of, these differences, the two men remained friends for decades (with a breach from the late 1790s until 1812). And, in the Second Continental Congress, they were staunch allies.

Independence dominated Congress's agenda. On June 7, 1776, Richard Henry Lee proposed three resolutions framed by the Virginia convention. The first proclaimed "that these united colonies are, and of right ought to be, free and independent states; that they are absolved from allegiance to the British crown, and that all political connection between them and the state of Great Britain is, and ought to be, totally dissolved." The second called for "articles of confederation and perpetual union" among the 13 colonies; the third urged Congress to send envoys to France and other European powers to find allies against Britain. The pressure of events made the time right for debating independence. Congress had reason to think that Americans would accept, and maybe welcome, steps that had seemed dangerous only a year before.

Congress named three committees to consider Lee's resolutions. The first was to prepare draft articles of confederation; the second was to plan American diplomatic efforts to win European allies; and the third was to draft a declaration of independence. It would be the last of a series of declarations by which the First and Second Continental Congresses had explained and defended the evolving American position in the constitutional argument with Britain.

In selecting the declaration committee, Congress balanced New England, the middle colonies, and the South. Because Lee had to return to Virginia, Congress named Jefferson in his place; also, Congress wanted to draw on what Adams (in his autobiography) called Jefferson's "happy talent for composition and singular felicity of expression." As independence's chief backer, Adams was a natural addition, as was Franklin, who brought his eminence and his diplomatic experience to the table. The influential Roger Sherman of Connecticut (Jefferson called him odd in manner but honest) and the diplomatic Robert R. Livingston of New York completed the roster.

According to Adams's autobiography, written in 1805, the committee named Adams and Jefferson as a subcommittee, and Adams talked Jefferson into preparing the draft:

> Mr. Jefferson desired me to...make the Draught. This I declined and gave several reasons for declining. 1. That he was a Virginian and I a Massachusettensian. 2. That he was a southern Man and I a northern one. 3. That I had been so obnoxious for my early and constant Zeal in promoting the Measure, that any draught of mine, would undergo a more severe Scrutiny and Criticism in Congress, than one of his composition. 4thly and lastly that would be reason enough if there were no other, I had a great Opinion of the Elegance of his pen and none at all of my own.... He accordingly...in a day or to produced to me his Draught....

By contrast, Jefferson recalled in a letter to James Madison written on August 20, 1823, that the committee "unanimously pressed on myself alone to make the draught." Jefferson probably was right that the committee argued him into drafting the Declaration, but Adams was correct in remembering the arguments he used to persuade Jefferson.

Jefferson closeted himself in his rooms in the boarding house owned by the bricklayer Jacob Graff Jr. Over the next 17 days, he drafted the Declaration, drawing heavily on the preamble to his draft constitution for Virginia. While he worked, he maintained his habit of recording each day's temperature and weather conditions, and he found the time to make purchases for Martha. Then he showed his draft to the other members of the committee. Only Adams and Franklin had major comments, and Jefferson added their suggestions to the draft that the committee presented to Congress on June 28, 1776.

In the 1820s, as the 50th anniversary of American independence loomed, controversy raged over how original the Declaration of Independence had been and who played what roles in framing it. On May 8, 1825, writing to Henry Lee, Jefferson explained that his purpose had been

> Not to find out new principles, or new arguments, never before thought of, not merely to say things which had never been said before; but to place before mankind the common sense of the subject, in terms so plain and firm as to command their assent, and to justify ourselves in the independent stand we are compelled to take. Neither aiming at originality of principle or sentiment, nor yet copied from any particular and previous writing, it was intended to be an expression of the American mind, and to give to that expression the proper tone and spirit called for by the occasion.

The Declaration blended the forward-looking thought of the Age of Enlightenment with hard-edged American constitutional and legal arguments. For example, its preamble set forth arguments about the natural rights of human

This page of Jefferson's rough draft of the Declaration of Independence shows his habitually neat penmanship, his concern for the visual attractiveness and the substantive content of his manuscripts, and his painstaking struggles to find the right words to capture ideas and arguments.

beings, devised by the 17th-century English philosopher John Locke, to lay the ground for invoking the right of revolution against a tyrant, the stated purpose of the Declaration. Jefferson also hoped to state the values by which Americans would govern themselves. Thus, the Declaration looked both backward, as the last word in the American argument

"ALL MEN ARE CREATED EQUAL"

Jefferson listed his writing of the Declaration of Independence as the first of three achievements "by which I wish most to be remembered." That document's opening paragraphs stated the core principles of the new American nation.

When in the course of human events it becomes necessary for one people to dissolve the political bands which have connected them with another, and to assume among the powers of the earth the separate and equal station to which the laws of nature and of nature's God entitle them, a decent respect to the opinions of mankind requires that they should declare the causes which impel them to the separation.

We hold these truths to be self-evident: that all men are created equal; that they are endowed by their creator with certain inalienable rights; that among these are life, liberty, and the pursuit of happiness: that to secure these rights, governments are instituted among men, deriving their just powers from the consent of the governed; that whenever any form of government becomes destructive of these ends, it is the right of the people to alter and abolish it, and to institute new government, laying its foundation on such principles, and organizing its powers in such form, as to them shall seem most likely to effect their safety and happiness. Prudence, indeed, will dictate that Governments long established should not be changed for light and transient causes; and accordingly all experience hath shewn, that mankind are more disposed to suffer, while evils are sufferable, than to right themselves by abolishing the forms to which they are accustomed. But when a long train of abuses and usurpations, pursuing invariably the same Object evinces a design to reduce them under absolute Despotism, it is their right, it is their duty, to throw off such Government, and to provide new Guards for their future security. . . .

with Britain, and forward, as a statement of the principles of American experiments in government. In 1776, most Americans focused on the charges against George III, each grounded in American views of the English constitution.

Jefferson was proud of his draft, but Congress saw the need to edit it. The delegates improved the Declaration considerably, sharpening its argument and keeping its focus on George III. The king had been the Americans' last court of appeal, but he had rejected their plea and launched a war to conquer them. By these actions, he had violated his coronation oath to do justly to all his subjects, and thus cut the last link binding Americans to Britain. The Declaration had to make this point clearly. Therefore, Congress cut Jefferson's eloquent paragraph scolding Parliament and the British people for not heeding American arguments.

The most controversial passage that Congress deleted blamed slavery and the slave trade on George III. It is not clear why Jefferson thought this charge justified, for many delegates owned slaves and had no desire to limit slavery, let alone abolish it. Jefferson himself owned more than 100 slaves; one of them, his valet Bob, was with him in Philadelphia. He also knew that, for decades, Virginia and the other colonies had enacted laws authorizing slavery, protecting slaveholders' property, and regulating the slave trade. British monarchs had to approve those statutes before they could become law, but the Crown did not bear all or even most of the blame for slavery. Jefferson may have hoped that attacking slavery in the Declaration might answer British opponents of the American cause, who ridiculed demands for liberty made by slaveholders. Congress, however, saw the passage as irrelevant and dangerous, a fatal flaw in the Declaration's case for independence, and they struck it out.

Jefferson took each cut as a personal affront. Franklin tried to ease his hurt feelings by telling him a story: A young man completes his apprenticeship as a hatter and drafts a sign for his shop: "John Thompson, Hatter, Makes and Sells

John Trumbull's The Declaration of Independence *shows the Declaration committee presenting its draft to the Second Continental Congress. The members of the committee are (left to right) John Adams, Robert R. Livingston, Roger Sherman, Thomas Jefferson, and Benjamin Franklin.*

Hats for Ready Money," with the picture of a hat. To be sure that he has the right text before having his sign painted, he shows it to friends. Each suggests cutting a word or phrase, giving good reasons for each cut, until all that is left is "John Thompson" and the picture of a hat. As Jefferson noted, Thompson's experience taught Franklin to "[make] it a rule, whenever in my power, to avoid becoming the draughtsman of papers to be reviewed by a public body."

Franklin's story amused Jefferson, who recorded it in his papers with other Franklin anecdotes, but it did not soothe his ruffled feathers. He sent friends copies of his draft, marked to indicate Congress's changes, hoping to prove that his draft was better than the final version. In 1821, when writing his autobiography, he included his draft for posterity.

Congress went forward on two tracks, one focusing on independence and the other on the document that would announce independence. On July 2, 1776, Congress adopted Lee's resolutions. Two days later, on July 4, Congress approved the Declaration. There was no formal signing ceremony.

Only John Hancock, the president of Congress, and Charles Thomson, the secretary of Congress, signed the Declaration at first. Over the course of more than a year, other delegates put their names to the document.

In 1776, few delegates in Congress, including Jefferson, foresaw the Declaration's pivotal role in American thought. They stressed the decision to declare independence, not the document explaining that act. In fact, not until 1784 was it publicly revealed that Jefferson had drafted the Declaration. However, as the states framed new constitutions, many cited the Declaration as authority for that step. And, after the young nation won its independence, Americans put the Declaration at the focus of their celebrations. By the 1820s, it had become the key document of American principles, out-ranking even the Constitution of the United States, a status it holds to this day. As a result, the Declaration carried Jefferson with it, enshrining the soft-spoken draftsman as the author of the central statement of the American political creed.

THE HARD WORK OF REVOLUTION (1776–1784)

Once the Second Continental Congress declared independence, it and the new state governments it had called into being took up the hard work of revolution. Congress had to learn to become a new nation's central institution of government. So, too, each former colony had to establish a new, legitimate form of government, and to turn itself into a "free and independent state." And Americans had to learn how to conduct politics, both within each state and on a new, untried national level.

Tackling the hard work of revolution, Thomas Jefferson learned difficult lessons about the conflict between framing idealistic measures and carrying them into effect. He also faced a greater challenge: striking a balance between his dedication to the Revolution (and his political career) and his devotion to his wife and family. These years gave Jefferson his greatest chance for creative statesmanship, but also brought him humiliation and disillusionment. Wounded, he turned his back on politics and retreated to his family, his plantation, and his books. Only a shattering personal tragedy spurred him to reenter public life.

The era of the Revolution was an age of experiments in government, focusing on the framing of new state constitutions.

Like John Adams, Jefferson hoped to make his mark as a constitution-maker. In June 1776, while preparing to draft the Declaration of Independence, he framed a new constitution for Virginia. Proudly, he sent his draft to Williamsburg with George Wythe, but Wythe arrived too late for the delegates to use it in devising the state's new government. Even so, they grafted onto their constitution Jefferson's preamble stating the case against George III and calling for independence.

In September 1776, Jefferson left Congress and returned to Virginia. On his return, he was elected to the Virginia legislature's lower house (renamed the House of Delegates) and shifted his attention from constitution-making to legal reform. This subject engaged his energies as an able lawyer and a devoted advocate of the Revolution's ideals. Virginia's laws, he argued, were a hodgepodge of statutes spanning nearly two centuries. Because most of these laws were not just old-fashioned but were relics of Virginia's colonial past under English kings, they were unfit to be the laws of a free people living under a republican government. Jefferson believed that the Revolution offered a priceless chance to reform or to abolish legal barriers to the individual's "pursuit of happiness" and the good of society.

First, he targeted the doctrine of entail. Rooted in English law, entail gave a property owner the power to require that only his direct descendants could inherit his land. Its purpose was to keep the land in the family, reinforcing aristocratic families' economic and social position. Anyone seeking to lift entail's restrictions from a property had to persuade the legislature to pass a law to "break the entail," an expensive, time-consuming procedure. Arguing that a property owner should be free to sell or bequeath his land to anyone, Jefferson persuaded the Virginia legislature to abolish entail.

Jefferson then proposed that Virginia frame a new code of laws. To undertake this task, the most ambitious program of law reform in America, the legislature named a five-member Committee of Revisors. Of these, the planters George Mason and Thomas Ludwell Lee stepped aside because, not being lawyers, they were not qualified for the task. Thus, the labor fell on Jefferson, George Wythe, and Edmund Pendleton.

Wythe and Pendleton were longtime foes whose legal clashes were legendary. Wythe shared Jefferson's enthusiasm for legal reform, but Pendleton preferred to defend established custom. One of Jefferson's chief targets—the common-law doctrine of primogeniture—was dear to Pendleton, a master of the old land law. Primogeniture required that, if a landowner had not made a will directing who should get his property, the oldest son would get the whole estate. Like entail, primogeniture spurred the rise of landed families, which, again, was why Jefferson insisted that it had no place in Virginia. Instead, he argued, even if a landowner died without leaving a will, the law should divide his estate equally among his children.

In a last-ditch attempt to save primogeniture, Pendleton proposed that the oldest son receive a share of the estate twice the size of that given to each of his brothers and sisters. Jefferson answered that this rule would make sense only if the oldest son needed to eat twice as much as his brothers and sisters. Stung by this retort, Pendleton confessed defeat, and the committee approved Jefferson's bill abolishing primogeniture.

Law reform captivated Jefferson. His proposals for revising Virginia's laws are our first clues to his vision of a good society, a happy and virtuous republic. First, he stressed reforming the criminal law. Virginia's laws were as harsh as the laws of England, which in the 18th century punished 300 separate crimes by death. Thus, in his Bill for Proportioning Crimes and Punishments, Jefferson set out to lift the death penalty from a host of crimes.

Jefferson also tried to reshape Virginia by framing new laws as well as by reforming old ones. He hoped, for example, to establish an elaborate system of public education—the first in America. The root of his Bill for the More General

Diffusion of Knowledge was his belief that citizens who hoped to govern themselves had to be educated.

First, he proposed to divide Virginia into sections called wards, each with a primary school for all male children. Each ward would send the one or two most gifted graduates of its primary school to the next level, a county school. Each county school would select its best graduate to go to the university, which Jefferson intended to have no ties with any religion or religious group. Though this bill never won the legislature's support, Jefferson proposed it repeatedly for the rest of his life.

Just as the Revolution's ideals clashed with slavery's persistence in the United States, Jefferson's efforts as a law reformer collided with his views of slavery and race. British writers denounced Americans for keeping slaves while demanding independence and liberty for themselves, and British generals promised slaves freedom if they ran away from their owners and joined in suppressing the Revolution. (They were inconsistent in keeping that promise, but that reality emerged only after the war's end.) Some Americans, such as Colonel John Laurens of South Carolina, an aide to General George Washington, urged their states to adopt similar policies to bolster the Continental Army, but to no avail.

Jefferson always was ambivalent about slavery. He opposed slavery in principle as an offense against human beings' natural rights—but other issues tangled with slavery in ways that drained his reforming energies. One source of his ambivalence may have been a lesson that he learned as a young politician. In 1769, he discussed with a senior lawmaker, Colonel Richard Bland, a bill permitting slaveholders to free their slaves (manumission). Bland offered to propose this manumission bill, which Jefferson would second. Bland's colleagues tore into him, publicly and privately, for proposing the bill; witnessing his ordeal left Jefferson wary of expressing opposition to slavery.

Jefferson had deeper reasons for his conflicted views of slavery than reluctance to risk his colleagues' hostility. For him, the racial differences separating whites and blacks were centrally important. Because, in his view, those differences defined whites as superior and blacks as inferior, he believed that blacks could not be trusted with freedom. Also, though he hoped to end slavery, he feared that former slaves' resentment of their past treatment would combine with former masters' fears of retribution to trigger a horrific race war. Because, as he saw it, whites and blacks could not live side by side in peace, he insisted that if slavery were abolished, the law must also command freed blacks to leave Virginia.

Revising Virginia's slave code, the committee made it harsher than before—for example, forbidding slaves or free blacks to testify in court against whites, and toughening penalties for crimes committed by slaves. The legislature rejected their most severe proposals, however, and in 1782 enacted a law establishing the procedures by which a master could free a slave. Until the law was tightened in 1806, a number of Virginia slaveholders freed slaves under this manumission law—but Jefferson never did.

In his autobiography, Jefferson claimed that his plans for law reform included a plan for general emancipation. The draft survives in his papers, but we have no evidence that his colleagues considered or even saw it. Even had they adopted it, his plan still would have continued slavery in Virginia for decades, and still would have forced all freed slaves to leave the state. Like many other slaveholders, he could not or would not grow beyond his origins as a member of the planter aristocracy; nor did he confront the agonizing contradiction between slavery's realities and the Revolution's ideals.

Jefferson thought that the greatest challenge his law-reform campaign faced was to define the proper relationship between church and state. Almost from its founding in 1607, Virginia had an established church—the Church of England (known in America, after 1776, as the Episcopal Church, for the Greek word for "bishop," stressing the central role of bishops in its chain of command). In a land with an established church, the government can force the people to attend that church's services—or pay fines for not doing so—and to pay money for its support, and the church teaches obedience to the government.

Virginia's established church sparked controversy even before the Revolution. Many ministers were lazy and corrupt, caring only that their salaries were paid regularly and that they received special grants of land in addition to their salaries. These privileges were widely unpopular, as was the Church's insistence that the law punish members of minority, or "dissenting," sects, such as Presbyterians and Baptists. For these reasons, as well as the Church's support of Britain in the years before 1776, the Revolution severely weakened the Episcopal Church's position in Virginia.

Allied against the Episcopal Church were religious dissenters and liberal Episcopalians such as George Mason, the principal draftsman of Virginia's Declaration of Rights. That document, adopted with the state's 1776 constitution, staked a powerful claim for religious liberty, but in terms that echoed the old practice of toleration. "Toleration" means that the majority allows a minority to worship in its own way, but only as a favor that the majority can take back for any reason.

Jefferson believed something different: that no majority, however strong or however true and good its religion, has a right to impose its views on anyone, even someone who believes in no religion at all. Beginning in the late 1760s, he differed with most Virginians—and most Americans—in religious belief. He embraced deism, the view that God had created the universe to run according to fixed, unchanging laws and therefore was not involved in people's daily lives. Jefferson kept his beliefs to himself; all his life, he was reluctant to reveal his views on religion to anyone except his closest friends. The only opinion on religion that he voiced in public was that an individual's views on religion should be the business only of that individual and God—and not the business of government.

For these reasons, Jefferson drafted his most sweeping law reform, the one central to his vision of a just society and closest to his heart. His Bill for Establishing Religious Freedom declared that government has no right to dictate what anyone can believe in matters of religion. In particular, his bill rejected any claim by government to tax individuals to support a specific religion or even the general cause of religion. It concluded with a defiant declaration that, although any later legislature might repeal this statute, its repeal would be "a violation of natural right."

Jefferson was proud of his work on law reform, and of his Bill for Establishing Religious Freedom most of all. Unfortunately for his project, the legislature ignored the sheaf of bills over which he, Wythe, and Pendleton had labored. Although they passed a few of his bills, most of the 126 proposals remained in the pages of the revisors' draft report, gathering dust in the General Assembly's files.

As Jefferson was completing his work on revising Virginia's laws, his friends prepared to win for him the state's highest office. On June 1, 1779, the legislature elected Jefferson, then 36 years old, as Virginia's second governor. Jefferson, his boyhood friend John Page, and General Thomas Nelson, the commander of the state militia, competed to succeed Patrick Henry, who had served three one-year terms and was barred from a fourth. On the first ballot, Jefferson had a strong lead over Page (but failed to win a majority), and Nelson came in a distant third; Page threw his support to Jefferson, who won on the second ballot. Jefferson's victory signaled the triumph of Virginia's radical reformers and showed that the state's politicians were more comfortable with the leadership of a gentleman planter than with the rough-and-tumble social climbing they associated with Patrick Henry.

Jefferson's governorship taught him humbling lessons about politics and governing. Neither he nor his fellow lawmakers considered whether he had the abilities of a successful

"ALMIGHTY GOD HATH CREATED THE MIND FREE"

Jefferson's greatest achievement as a lawmaker was Virginia's Bill for Religious Freedom (drafted in 1779), which denied government any power to dictate what the individual should believe in matters of religion. James Madison convinced his fellow lawmakers to enact it in 1786.

Well aware that the opinions and belief of men depend not on their own will but follow involuntarily the evidence proposed to their minds; that Almighty God hath created the mind free, and manifested his supreme will that free it shall remain by making it altogether insusceptible of restraint; that all attempts to influence it by corporal punishments, or burthens, or by civil incapacitations, tend only to beget habits of hypocrisy and meanness, and are a departure from the plan of the holy author of our religion, who being lord both of body and mind, yet chose not to propagate it by coercions on either, as was in his Almighty power to do, but to extend it by its influence on reason alone; that the impious presumption of legislators and rulers, civil as well as ecclesiastical, who, being themselves but fallible and uninspired men, have assumed dominion over the faith of others, setting up their own opinions and modes of thinking as the only true and infallible his right infallible, and as such endeavoring to impose them on others, hath established and maintained false religions over the greatest part of the world and through all time: That to compel a man to furnish contributions of money for the propagation of opinions which he disbelieves and abhors, is sinful and tyrannical; that even the forcing him to support this or that teacher of his own religious persuasion, is depriving him of the comfortable liberty of giving his contributions to the particular pastor whose morals he would make his pattern, and whose powers he feels most persuasive to righteousness....

chief executive. The situation when he took office complicated his problems. The heady early days of the Revolution were long past. By 1779, it had become a grim civil war; Patriot forces (the Continental Army and state militias) fought British and Loyalist forces, with some French support for the Americans and with Native American nations' warriors occasionally taking part on both sides. It was hard to rouse the people to support the cause of freedom and independence, and Jefferson not only was reluctant to coerce them but naively believed that coercion would not be needed.

Governor Jefferson deferred to the legislature. He forged cordial working relationships with the General Assembly and with his Council of State, which acted as the legislature's upper house and as an executive advisory committee. He needed their support, because the war was Virginia's dominant problem. Even the only other major issue of state politics in 1779–80, the location of the state's capital, was shaped by concerns over the war: Should the capital leave Williamsburg, which was vulnerable to enemy attack, for the more central town of Richmond? Jefferson backed Richmond, in part because he loathed Williamsburg's architecture and thirsted to help shape Richmond's development. He also found this task a welcome distraction from overseeing the state's response to the war's demands.

Administrative burdens dominated Jefferson's time and absorbed his energies; he had to deal with an unending stream of paperwork, but he had almost no power. He persuaded the legislature to create two departments to assist him, one for finance and one for defense. However, he still was caught between two conflicting sets of demands. The Continental Congress and the Continental Army begged Virginia (the Union's largest state) for money, men, and supplies; Virginians, fearing that they were a prime target for invasion, insisted on keeping resources for their own defense. Jefferson tried his best, but his lack of authority hampered him at every turn. So did his excessive faith that Virginians would spring to their state's defense without having to be organized for the purpose or ordered to do so.

Jefferson was reelected as governor in June 1780. Unfortunately, December 1779 had brought an omen of trouble. A British naval expedition sailed south from New York City, bypassed Virginia, and headed for Charleston, South Carolina, to support the British capture of that city. The British were shifting their focus southward. In December 1780, a British army led by the traitor Benedict Arnold invaded Virginia; in January 1781, a naval landing force positioned Arnold's army for operations in the heart of the state. By this time, the state government had moved from Williamsburg to Richmond—but Richmond was Arnold's target. That winter, Jefferson oversaw the government's evacuation from the city; Arnold briefly seized Richmond and withdrew, spreading alarm through Virginia.

In the spring of 1781, Lord Charles Cornwallis took command of British forces in Virginia. The Marquis de Lafayette's 1,200 Continental soldiers were no match for Cornwallis's 7,200 disciplined regulars. Lafayette could only harass Cornwallis's forces and retreat out of harm's way, annoying the British. In May 1781, heeding reports that Cornwallis planned to capture Richmond again, Jefferson and the legislature relocated to Charlottesville, near Monticello.

The events of May and June 1781 became the low point of Jefferson's governorship and his public career. On May 31, 1781, Cornwallis sent a swift cavalry column sweeping into the heart of Virginia. Its commander, Lieutenant Colonel Banastre Tarleton, hoped to capture the state government. Unprepared for this threat, Jefferson and his colleagues had done nothing to organize armed resistance, in part because Jefferson believed that Virginians would rise up of their own accord to repel the foe. Jack Jouett, a Virginia cavalryman, saw Tarleton's men beginning their advance and galloped 40 miles overnight at breakneck speed to warn the governor. Coolly, Jefferson rode out on horse-back to assess the situation. Then he supervised the government's evacuation to Staunton, and waited until his wife and children were safely away. Only then did he leave, avoiding capture by a British cavalry detachment. Tarleton took and held Monticello and Charlottesville for a few days, and retreated. A few of Jefferson's slaves ran away, hoping to find liberty; Jefferson later charged that Virginia lost tens of thousands of slaves during the Revolution, due to British promises that slaves who deserted their masters would receive liberty.

Up to this point, Governor Jefferson had done as well responding to the crisis as anyone could expect. His term as governor had expired on June 2, 1781, and he had decided not to seek a third term. The legislature had postponed the election of his successor for 10 days; thus, when Tarleton's forces reached Charlottesville on June 4, Jefferson was act-ing as governor even after his term was over. Once Jefferson had carried out his duties, however, his literal-minded approach to government caused him to make a serious error. With the crisis passed, he saw himself as a private citi-zen once more, and rejoined his family at Poplar Forest (a plantation that he and his wife had inherited from her father), instead of going to Staunton to turn over the reins of power to his successor.

Jefferson thus left Virginia without a governor between June 4 and June 12, when the Assembly chose General Nelson to succeed him. His actions astonished many Virginians, and some were not in a forgiving frame of mind. On June 12, George Nicholas demanded an investigation of the conduct of the state's executive, a shot aimed at Jefferson and at his Council of State. Accusations of cow-ardice against Jefferson flew through Virginia, wounding him deeply; the news that Patrick Henry supported Nicholas's resolution worsened the breach between the Henry and Jefferson factions.

The legislature scheduled the probe to begin on December 12, 1781. In October, at the battle of Yorktown, on Virginia's eastern coast, a French-American force commanded by Washington defeated Cornwallis and captured his army. Yorktown, a pivotal moment in the war, changed the state's political climate. At this time, the delegate for Jefferson's county of Albemarle resigned, and Jefferson won election to the seat. On December 12, when the inquiry was to begin, Nicholas did not even show up. When no one else raised the subject, Jefferson claimed the floor and answered the charges against him point by point. It was a notable performance, given his strong dislike for public speaking. Embarrassed, the legislature cleared him of all charges and adopted resolutions thanking him for his service—after which he resigned his seat.

Afterward, Jefferson swore that he was through with public life, insisted that he had suffered too much in public service to undertake it again, and denied that he had any further obligation to answer his country's call. On May 20, 1782, for example, he vented his bitterness to James Monroe, who had been elected to the legislature and hoped that he and Jefferson could work together: "I felt that these injuries, for such they since have been acknowledged had inflicted a wound on my spirit which only will be cured by the all-healing grave."

Despite Jefferson's sense of injury, some good came of his governorship. In particular, he formed three friendships—with James Madison, James Monroe, and William Short—that sustained him, personally and politically, for the rest of his life. Like Jefferson, all three men were members of the planter elite, but in other ways they were quite different from one another.

Jefferson and Madison had first met in 1776, when Jefferson returned from the Second Continental Congress to take his seat in the Virginia legislature; but not until 1779, when Madison was named to Governor Jefferson's

Council of State, did they form a close, lasting friendship. Quiet and retiring, Madison was eight years younger than Jefferson. About five feet five inches tall, he was so slight in build that one observer joked that he must have been carved from a piece of soap. He had thinning reddish-brown hair, which he brushed back and powdered, in the custom of the day. Powdering hair gave an appearance of age and gravity, which Madison needed, because until he was in his fifties he seemed far younger than his age.

Unlike most Virginia gentlemen, including Jefferson, who were educated at William and Mary, Madison had attended the College of New Jersey (now Princeton). There, he received a superb education, supervised by the Scottish-born Rev. John Witherspoon, the college's president and one of the greatest educators of his time. Madison stayed an extra year after earning his college degree, studying history, ethics, moral philosophy, and Hebrew. He was unsure what career he should pursue. His frail health depressed him, for he did not believe that he had the energy or fixed purpose to enter the clergy or to practice law.

The Revolution helped Madison to find a calling—politics. At the Virginia convention of 1776, he helped George Mason to frame the religious liberty clauses of Virginia's Declaration of Rights. Soon after, the prim, proper Madison made his only major misstep as a politician; he did not treat the voters of his district to free drinks, and he was defeated at the polls. He learned his lesson, and never again lost an election.

Madison and Jefferson had much in common. Both were hardworking legislators, skilled at drafting laws and serving on committees, and both had weak voices that failed to carry across a legislative chamber. Unlike Jefferson, however, Madison was a skilled and convincing speaker; when he took the floor, his colleagues would gather around him to hear him better. The two men had similar intellectual habits and political views. Both were devoted readers; both were committed to religious liberty, separation of church and state, and protecting Virginia's interests. They formed a partnership of equals. Jefferson deeply respected Madison, recognized that he had a powerful and learned mind, and often heeded his advice. From 1776 until Jefferson's death in 1826, Madison was the only man Jefferson would listen to when he disagreed with Jefferson and pointed out flaws in his ideas.

Like Madison, James Monroe was younger than Jefferson. Unlike Madison, Monroe did not have a powerful or learned mind, but he had other qualities that Jefferson admired. Born in 1758, he was a veteran of the Revolution, a war hero whose bravery was a cornerstone of his political career. Educated at William and Mary, he was more typical of that college's graduates than Jefferson was. He was outgoing though slightly stiff in manner, and passionate in defense of his honor. Jefferson guided Monroe's study of law and was his sponsor when Monroe joined the Virginia bar. Jefferson valued Monroe for what he described as the purity of his character, writing to William Temple Franklin (grandson of Benjamin Franklin) on May 7, 1786, "[Monroe] is a man whose soul might be turned wrong side outwards without discovering a blemish to the world."

William Short, born in 1759, was a relative by marriage of Jefferson, and, like Jefferson and Monroe, an alumnus of William and Mary. In 1779, Short attended the first public law lectures in America, given by George Wythe. Wythe became Short's mentor, and Jefferson was one of Short's examiners when he was admitted to the bar. Short took on Jefferson as a client, doing legal work for the estate of John Wayles. Jefferson thought of Short as his "adoptive son"; he wrote to Madison that Short had "a peculiar talent for prying into facts." Short launched his legal practice in Richmond and soon was named to the Council of State. In the 1780s, he was Jefferson's secretary in Paris, and then pursued a diplomatic and business career.

For the rest of his life, Jefferson relied on Madison, Monroe, and Short, leaning on them for support, consulting with them, and guiding them in their shared purposes. They formed a core of trusted friends, advisers, and allies, even when they occasionally differed with one another.

In late 1781, however, Jefferson sought to convince everyone, including his closest friends, that he was finished with public life. He was determined to spend the rest of his days with his family, living as a gentleman planter. To occupy his mind, he took up an intellectual project left over from his governorship. In 1780, the French diplomat François Barbé-Marbois had sent a questionnaire to the governors of all 13 states, seeking information about each state's geography, natural resources, history, law, politics, and economy. Only a few bothered to reply. Now, Jefferson dug out the questionnaire and wrote a book-length manuscript, modestly titled *Notes on the State of Virginia*. He devoted a chapter, or "Query," to each of the Frenchman's questions, but reshuffled them into an order that suited him.

Writing *Notes* gave Jefferson the chance to reflect on Virginia and to ponder what Europeans wanted to know about America. It also gave him a platform to hold forth on his most cherished ideas and interests, such as religious liberty, the proper structure of a constitution, the virtues of the native peoples of America, and agriculture as the best way of life for a free people wishing to remain free. Jefferson was beginning to frame a full-dress statement of his vision of a good society, one based on honest farmers, republican government, honest and simple manners, and devotion to liberty. Before the end of 1781 he set the unfinished manuscript aside, planning to return to it later.

Martha Wayles Jefferson used this bell to summon servants. Hemings family tradition relates that Sally, who helped her mother, Betty Hemings, tend the dying wife of Thomas Jefferson, was given this bell as a memento after Martha's death.

Jefferson's friends refused to accept his decision to retire from politics. Regularly, Congress offered him assignments, but he always declined. His wife was expecting a child, and the evidence suggests that he feared leaving his wife's side during her pregnancy, but he was reluctant to explain himself even to trusted friends. His silence persuaded such politicians as Richard Henry Lee that he was selfishly putting private happiness ahead of public duty, and they began to cool towards him.

On April 13, 1782, Jefferson's 39th birthday, François Jean, Marquis de Chastellux, visited Monticello. In his account of his travels, Chastellux penned a superb brief portrait of Jefferson:

> Let me describe to you a man not yet forty, tall, and with a mild pleasing countenance, but whose mind and understanding are ample substitutes for every exterior grace. An American who without ever quitting his country, is at once a musician, skilled in drawing, a geometrician,

an astronomer, a natural philosopher, legislator, and statesman; a senator of America who sat for two years in that famous Congress that brought about the revolution, and that is never mentioned without respect, though unhappily not without regret; a Governor of Virginia who filled this difficult station during the invasions of Arnold, of Phillips, and of Cornwallis; a philosopher in voluntary retirement from the world and public business, because he loves the world inasmuch only as he can flatter himself with being useful to mankind: and the minds of his countrymen are not yet in a condition either to bear the light or to suffer contradiction; a mild and amiable wife, charming children, of whose education he himself takes charge, a house to embellish, great provisions, and the arts and sciences to cultivate.... [I]t seems as if from his youth he had placed his mind, as he had done his house, on an elevated situation, from which he might contemplate the universe.

Chastellux also wrote a valuable early sketch of Monticello:

The house, of which Mr. Jefferson was the architect, and often the builder, is constructed in an Italian style, and is quite tasteful, although not however without some faults; it consists of a large square pavilion, into which one enters through two porticoes ornamented with columns. The ground floor consists chiefly of a large and lofty salon, or drawing room, which is to be decorated entirely in the antique style.... His house resembles none of the others seen in this country; so that it may be said that Mr. Jefferson is the first American who has consulted the Fine Arts to know how he should shelter himself from the weather.

Had Chastellux visited Virginia five months later, he would not have had a chance to record his impressions of Jefferson's "mild and amiable wife." In August 1782, Martha Jefferson gave birth to their sixth child, Lucy, and then fell ill. Her husband never left her side; they both knew that she was dying. Jefferson's overseer, Edmund Bacon, and descendants of Sally Hemings, who as a child was one of the slaves attending Martha on her deathbed, reported that Martha made Thomas promise that he would not remarry, so that her children would not have to be raised by a stepmother, as she had been.

On September 6, 1782, Martha Wayles Skelton Jefferson died, aged 34. Childbirth, always an ordeal for mothers in this era, was especially hard for her. In her 10 years with Jefferson, she had given birth to five daughters and one son (who died after a few weeks); in addition, with her first husband, she had had one son, who died in 1773, the year after her remarriage. Only Martha, Maria, and Lucy survived her.

Jefferson collapsed under the strain of Martha's illness and death. In his wife's last moments, his sister Martha Carr instructed his slaves to carry him, half-fainting with grief, to his room. She feared that, if he were present at Martha's death, the shock would kill him too. For weeks he was delirious. After he left his sickbed, he roamed the grounds of Monticello, sometimes on horseback but more often on foot, with his nine-year-old daughter Martha as his only companion. In these rambles he often gave way to his grief. He burned all of his wife's letters and papers—except one. On her deathbed, she had begun to copy a quotation about the death of a loved one from their favorite novel, Laurence Sterne's *Tristram Shandy*, but she had been too weak to complete it, and he finished it for her. Now he kept that lone scrap of her writing, folded around a lock of her hair, locked in a secret compartment of his desk.

This paper is one of the few surviving manuscripts in the handwriting of Martha Jefferson, who died at the age of 34 after complications from childbirth. Only one of the six children she had with Thomas Jefferson survived both her and her husband.

In late 1782, Congress sought to lure Jefferson from retirement, naming him, with John Adams, Benjamin Franklin, and John Jay, to the American delegation assigned to negotiate a peace treaty with Britain. (A fifth diplomat, South Carolina's Henry Laurens, had been captured by the British and was a prisoner in the Tower of London.) Had his wife been alive, Jefferson would have turned the appointment down. Now, this honor, and the chance to visit Europe, cut through the fog of his grief and helped revive his interest in affairs of the world. Before he could leave for Paris, however, word arrived that Jay, Franklin, and Adams had achieved more than anyone had dared to hope for. Under the Treaty of Paris of 1783, Britain recognized American independence and American fishing rights along the Canadian coast, and gave the United States all land between the Allegheny Mountains and the Mississippi River, doubling the new nation's size. Unfortunately, the treaty's completion scuttled Jefferson's plans to travel to Europe.

In June 1783, Virginia sent Jefferson to Philadelphia to lead the state's delegation to the Confederation Congress (the successor to the Second Continental Congress, under the Articles of Confederation). In Congress, Jefferson took special interest in the territories won from Britain. He had long recognized the potential for American expansion westward, and he was convinced that the West would be the key to defining the character of the new nation. He hoped to encourage the spread westward of a republic of individual farmers, each tilling his own land and committed to personal and national independence and liberty. For these reasons, Jefferson rejected the European system of colonialism—a mother country ruling its colonies in its own interest. Rather, he insisted, Congress should allow the new territories to govern themselves under its supervision.

Once each territory reached a set level of population, it could petition Congress to join the Union as a new state, equal in status to the original 13. Jefferson also proposed that surveyors of these new territories divide them into individual farm-sized plots of land, based on a rectangular grid. This plan, written by Congress into the Ordinance of 1785, continues to shape the Midwest and West to this day. Finally, Jefferson proposed to divide the territory into states with names he devised himself, drawing on his command of Greek and Latin and his interest in Native American languages.

Congress adopted Jefferson's vision of an expanding Union (but not his list of names), and in 1787 two American lawmaking bodies built on his work. The Confederation Congress enacted the Northwest Ordinance, the third and most famous of the three territorial ordinances it passed between 1784 and 1787, and the Federal Convention wrote the idea of creating new states into the United States Constitution.

Jefferson suffered one major defeat of his ideas about governing the territories, however. He had hoped to include in the 1784 Territorial Ordinance a ban on slavery in the new states, but the illness of one New Jersey delegate cost that state its vote, and his proposal was defeated. Jefferson lamented this lost opportunity, though such a measure would have had no direct effect on slavery in the original 13 states.

Jefferson's labors in Congress impressed his colleagues, and he remained a leading candidate to represent the United States abroad. When in 1784 Congress finally offered him another chance to undertake a diplomatic mission, Jefferson eagerly seized it and began one of the most creative and personally significant periods of his life.

CHAPTER

4

"BEHOLD ME AT LENGTH ON THE VAUNTED SCENE OF EUROPE!" (1784–1789)

On September 13, 1785, writing from Paris, Thomas Jefferson, the new American minister to France, confided his views of Europe to an old friend. The Italian scholar Charles Bellini had come to Virginia in 1773; in 1779, Jefferson helped to arrange for Bellini to become the first professor of modern languages at the College of William and Mary. Now Jefferson tried to express to Bellini the impressions that whirled through his mind:

> Behold me at length on the vaunted scene of Europe!...
> [Y]ou are, perhaps, curious to know how this new scene
> has struck a savage of the mountains of America. Not
> advantageously, I assure you. I find the general fate of
> humanity here, most deplorable. The truth of Voltaire's
> observation, offers itself perpetually, that every man here
> must be either the hammer or the anvil....

He insisted that the lives even of European aristocrats were "[m]uch, very much inferior... to the tranquil, perma-nent felicity with which domestic society in America, blesses most of its inhabitants." And yet he had to admit that he enjoyed European "pleasures of the table... because, with good taste they unite temperance," and he envied European fine arts:

Were I to proceed to tell you how much I enjoy their architecture, sculpture, painting, music, I should want words. It is in these arts they shine. The last of them, particularly, is an enjoyment, the deprivation of which with us, cannot be calculated. I am almost ready to say, it is the only thing which from my heart I envy them, and which, in spite of all the authority of the Decalogue, I do covet.

In little more than a year, Jefferson had transformed himself from a Virginia revolutionary and politician into an American diplomat. On May 7, 1784, the Confederation Congress named him, John Adams, and Benjamin Franklin to negotiate commercial treaties with European nations. On receiving word of his mission, Jefferson traveled from Monticello to Boston to book passage for Europe. His oldest daughter, Martha (nicknamed "Patsy"), accompanied him. On July 5, 1784, he and his party left for Paris on the ship *Ceres*. Four weeks later, on August 6, they reached France.

At first Jefferson was uncomfortable in his new setting. He had never visited so large a city before, and though he could read French, his grasp of the spoken language was shaky. Paris that winter was chill and damp, a far cry from Virginia's warmth and sunshine. He reported to friends that his health was suffering from the struggle to adapt to the climate. Just as he and Patsy were becoming used to being

At the left edge of this 18th-century engraving of Paris stands the Hotel de Langeac, which Jefferson rented while he was American minister to France. Jefferson cherished Paris's music, art, and culture but warned his countrymen against the corruption and dangers of urban life.

abroad, they received sorrowful news from home; in January 1785, French Marquis de Lafayette informed them that, two months before, Jefferson's youngest daughter, Lucy, had died of whooping cough at the age of two.

To distract himself from his loss, Jefferson threw himself into his work. Fortunately, he liked and respected his fellow negotiators; he was an effective balance between the urbane Franklin and the prickly, suspicious Adams, who disliked each other but agreed on their esteem for Jefferson. He became welcome in the Franklin household and an adopted member of the Adams family circle. In particular, Adams's brilliant wife Abigail befriended him and became deeply fond of Patsy. Because he was more comfortable in a domestic setting than in the social whirl of Parisian salons, Jefferson differed from Franklin and was more like the Adamses. For this reason, he spent much of his energy during his first year in Paris seeking a proper home for himself, his daughter, the slaves he had brought from Virginia, and the servants he had hired in Paris. He finally set on a house known as the Hotel de Langeac, where he lived for the rest of his tour of duty.

On May 2, 1785, Jefferson learned that Congress had agreed to Franklin's retirement as American minister to France and had named him to fill the post. Three weeks later, on May 23, John Adams left Paris with his family to take up his duties as American minister to Great Britain; and on July 15, Franklin began his journey home. Their departures left Jefferson on his own.

To meet the challenges of his new post, Jefferson drew on his experience in state and national politics. Certain aspects of his personality, notably his dislike of confrontation and his gift for the apt phrase, helped to ensure his success as a diplomat. For example, whenever he was presented as the new American minister to France and asked whether he was Franklin's replacement, he answered, "[N]o one can replace him, Sir: I am only his successor."

By contrast, his attempt to act as a diplomat in Britain (aiding Adams in seeking a treaty of commerce) failed, but through no fault of his own. When, on March 11, 1786, Adams presented Jefferson to George III, the English monarch, who still resented Jefferson's writings against him, snubbed the Virginian, in stark contrast to the friendly greeting that the king had given Adams when he had presented his credentials. As Jefferson recalled in his autobiography, "On my presentation as usual to the King and Queen at their levees, it was impossible for anything to be more ungracious than their notice of Mr. Adams & myself." George III's hostile treatment, echoed by that of the Foreign Ministry, helped to fan Jefferson's growing hostility to Britain.

Jefferson was impatient with the usual patterns of great-power diplomacy, particularly the stress on personal relations between kings, and on alliances founded on those relationships, and he had strong views of what policies would best serve American interests. Devoted to trade between nations unburdened by tariffs or commercial restrictions, he fought to establish free trade between the United States and European nations. Working with John Adams, he persuaded the king of Prussia to sign a commercial treaty with the United States based on free trade, and he hoped to negotiate similar pacts with other powers—even with Britain—but to no avail.

In November 1788, however, he negotiated a treaty, the Consular Convention of 1788, which governed activities of American diplomats in France and French diplomats in the United States. This was one of the first treaties ratified by the Senate in 1789 under the new Constitution of the United States.

Representing the United States in economic negotiations with government officials and private bankers in Paris and Amsterdam was Jefferson's greatest burden. Repeatedly, he had to renegotiate the terms of the loans that the United States had used to finance its war for independence. Usually he undertook these tasks on his own; sometimes, as when he visited the Netherlands in early 1788, he worked with Adams. Often he had to endure close, hostile questioning about the new nation's stability, its ramshackle finances, and its ability to repay its sizeable debts. Jefferson found this ordeal humiliating, especially as he recognized that one reason for American financial troubles was the Confederation government's lack of power.

Jefferson excelled in another diplomatic task—gathering intelligence. His extensive letters home supplied John Jay, the Confederation's secretary for foreign affairs, and other well-placed Americans (including Washington and Madison) with detailed information on European affairs and their consequences for the United States. He was a shrewd observer, skilled at amassing and sifting information from a variety of sources, both public and private. In particular, he used his friendships with such Frenchmen as the Marquis de Lafayette to ferret out information about the intentions of King Louis XVI and his ministers.

The tasks of an American diplomat abroad were demanding and sometimes frustrating, but they did not add up to a full-time job. Nonetheless, Jefferson found much to occupy him. Not only was he carrying out delicate fiscal and diplomatic assignments, he also was a visible symbol of the United States, an advocate of American interests, and an industrious observer of all things that might benefit his country. Giving free rein to his curiosity about Europe, he recorded his observations in travel diaries, reports, and letters. He also ransacked the Paris bookstalls for his own library and for the collection of James Madison, who swapped wish lists with him. In addition to books, he sought musical instruments and sheet music, for himself and for his daughters. All the while, he parried European questions about American conditions, reassured curious Europeans about his nation's stability, and promoted emigration to the United States.

One of Jefferson's most engrossing projects was his campaign for American intellectual independence from

Europe. The arena that he chose was not governance or politics but nature. With his *Histoire Naturelle* (*Natural History*) in dozens of volumes, Georges-Louis Leclerc, comte de Buffon, had established himself as the Atlantic world's greatest expert on the subject. As a key theme of his book, Buffon asserted, without proof, that all plant and animal life, including human life, was smaller, weaker, and shorter-lived in America than in Europe. He built his claims on a tradition of European disdain for America going back more than two centuries.

Buffon's argument dismayed and angered Jefferson, because he knew it to be untrue and because he feared that such rumors would turn would-be immigrants away from America. Jefferson begged his friends to find animal specimens proving that nature did not favor the Old World at the expense of the New World; he presented these specimens— including pelts, elk and moose antlers, and stuffed animals— to Buffon.

Specimens were not enough, however; Jefferson knew that to refute a book, it was necessary to write a book. Therefore, at the same time that he was arranging to pile samples of American flora and fauna before Buffon, he dug out the manuscript that he had begun in 1781 to answer the queries posed by the French diplomat François Barbé-Marbois. Working quickly, he revised and expanded it, and it saw print in May 1785 under the title *Notes on the State of Virginia*.

At first, apparently because he feared that his comments on slavery and on the Virginia constitution would bring vehement criticism down on him, he directed that the first edition comprise only 200 copies, for friends in Europe and America, and he left his name off the title page. Unfortunately, a French publisher obtained a copy, cobbled together a fast translation, and planned to publish it with Jefferson's name splashed across the title page. Mortified, Jefferson decided to beat the pirating publisher at his own game, and he authorized two general editions of *Notes on the State of Virginia*. One was a French

1785
FIRST ISSUE

Lacking pp. 327-366.
MS corrections on 316-317.

322

Th. Jefferson having had a few copies of these Notes printed to offer to some of his friends & to some other estimable characters beyond that line, begs the Abbé Morellet's acceptance of a copy. unwilling to expose them to the public eye he asks the favour of the Abbé Morellet to put them into the hands of no person on whose care & fidelity he cannot rely to guard them against publication. —

Cette note est de la main de mr. Jefferson alors ministre plenipotentiaire des etats unis et depuis ministre + des affaires etrangeres dans son pays. Il a consenti qu'elle fut lui même a la production a ce que j'en fisse et que j'en publiasse la traduction. A Morellet

With bookplate of the abbé André Morellet whose translation of this work was printed at Paris in 1786.

NOTES on the state of VIRGINIA;

written in the year 1781, somewhat corrected and enlarged in the winter of 1782, for the use of a Foreigner of distinction, in answer to certain queries proposed by him respecting

MDCCLXXXII.

[Paris 1785]

The title page of the first, private edition of Notes on the State of Virginia *omits Jefferson's name. The* Notes *set forth Jefferson's eloquent vision of a good society—an independent republic of small farmers committed to liberty and republican government.*

translation prepared under his supervision by a liberal clergyman, the Abbé André Morellet, and published anonymously; the other, a revised edition in English by the London publisher John Stockdale, appeared in 1787, bearing Jefferson's name.

Notes on the State of Virginia, Jefferson's only full-dress literary performance, has been described as perhaps the most important American book published before 1800, an example of scholarship in the Age of Enlightenment. Addressing Virginia's geography, natural history and resources, agriculture, laws, governance, history, politics, religion, and social customs, it displays Jefferson's mastery of a dazzling spectrum of bodies of knowledge, which he synthesized to produce an eloquent, almost starry-eyed tribute to Virginia and to America.

In *Notes,* Jefferson demolished Buffon's claims that nature and man degenerated in the New World, compiling tables of statistics to prove that plant and animal life in Virginia was equal to, if not richer than, European flora and fauna. In some of his most lyrical pages, he described Native Americans' virtues and talents, praising their courage and eloquence, and excusing what he called their primitive habits and customs as the products of ignorance; he also painted word pictures of such natural wonders as Virginia's Natural Bridge, which happened to be on land that he owned. Jefferson also sketched the Virginia constitution, hailing its virtues and damning its faults, such as its concentration of power in the legislature, in pages that continued to stir controversy in Virginia more than 40 years later.

Jefferson's devotion to liberty and equality stopped short when he wrote of slavery and race. By this time, he had reached an uneasy balance in his mind on slavery. He still denounced the institution in harsh, bitter terms. In Query XVIII, "Manners," he exploded in despair:

> And can the liberties of a nation be thought secure when we have removed their only firm basis, a conviction in the minds of the people that these liberties are of the gift of God? That they are not to be violated but with his wrath? Indeed I tremble for my country when I reflect that God is just: that his justice cannot sleep for ever: that considering numbers, nature and natural means only, a revolution of the wheel of fortune, an exchange of situation, is among possible events: that it may become probable by supernatural interference! The Almighty has no attribute which can take side with us in such a contest.

And yet, in Query XIV, "Laws," he struggled to explain why Virginia could not abolish slavery at once and why abolition required exiling all freed slaves from the state. He stressed the central difference between masters and slaves—that of race, or what he called "the real distinctions which nature has made" between whites and blacks. Jefferson claimed that Africans were inferior to Europeans, listing such differences as skin color, facial features, body type, and habits. But his list was not neutral or scientific, though he wrote as if it were. Rather, he skewed his results to tip the balance, every time, for whites and against blacks, cloaking his bias with the appearance of scientific impartiality:

> I advance it therefore as a suspicion only, that the blacks, whether originally a distinct race, or made distinct by time and circumstances, are inferior to the whites in the endowments both of body and mind. It is not against experience to suppose that different species of the same genus, or varieties of the same species, may possess different qualifications. Will not a lover of natural history then, one who views the gradations in all the races of animals with the eye of philosophy, excuse an effort to keep those in the department of man as distinct as nature has formed them? This unfortunate difference of colour, and perhaps of faculty, is a powerful obstacle to the emancipation of these people.

Jefferson's tortured defense of racial inequality horrifies modern readers. He helped to invent a new form of argument for racial inferiority, one invoking the authority of science. Later generations of white Americans used his words in Query XIV to justify slavery, while rejecting his arguments in Query XVIII, based on his ideas of natural law and natural rights, that slavery was wrong and damaging to whites and blacks alike. Thus, *Notes on the State of Virginia* exemplified both the most admirable and the most appalling sides of Jefferson's thought.

Jefferson's complex engagement with Europe had a personal as well as an intellectual dimension. While in Paris, he found his emotions stirred as they had not been since his wife's death. In the summer of 1786, the American artist John Trumbull, who had come to Paris to study art, introduced him to Maria Cosway. Like Martha Wayles Jefferson, Maria Cosway was short and slight; she had bright blue eyes and a mass of curly, elaborately styled blond hair. Born in Italy to English parents, she had studied art and won a modest reputation as a portrait painter. Her husband, the painter Richard Cosway, had brought her to Paris. Sixteen years Jefferson's junior, Maria dazzled him. For a time, they toured Paris together, visiting art galleries, public buildings, and classical ruins. On September 18, 1786, bubbling over with high spirits while walking with her, he tried to vault a low fence and fell, fracturing his right wrist and spraining his left. For months thereafter, he wrote painfully with his left hand.

It is not clear what happened between Thomas Jefferson and Maria Cosway, beyond a series of romantic afternoons touring Paris and the neighboring countryside. On October 12, 1786, he wrote her the longest letter of his life, an elaborate dialogue, half-flirtatious and half-philosophical, between his Head and his Heart. In this letter, drawing on the literary conventions of 18th-century letter writing, and echoing the literary games of his favorite novelist, Laurence Sterne, Jefferson presented an image of himself divided between his calculating, pragmatic Head and his honest, generous Heart, who in the following extract tells the Head to know its limits:

Maria Cosway captivated Jefferson when they met in 1786. Whether they pursued an extended flirtation or a doomed romance, Cosway touched Jefferson's heart for the first time since the death of his wife, Martha.

> When nature assigned us the same habitation, she gave us over it a divided empire. To you she allotted the field of science; to me that of morals.... In short, my friend, as far as my recollection serves me, I do not know that I ever did a good thing on your suggestion, nor a dirty one without it. I do forever then disclaim your interference in my province. Fill papers as you please with triangles & squares: try how many ways you can hang & combine them together. I shall never envy nor controul your sublime delights. But leave me to decide when & where friendships are to be contracted.

In her response, Maria praised the letter, regretting that she could write nothing to live up to it; but later, to her dismay, she realized that she was doing most of the letter writing and his responses were few and far between. In their relationship, first one and then the other was more aggressive and insistent.

One reason for this seesawing may have been their recognition that it was impossible for the relationship to progress beyond what it was. Maria was married, though unhappy with her husband, and a Roman Catholic who did not believe in divorce. Thus, she refused to break her marriage vows. Further, she was a European who could not imagine emigrating to or visiting America, despite Jefferson's repeated, broad hints to her on the subject, whereas he was an American who regarded his time in Europe only as a visit. Also, Jefferson was different from most men whom Maria knew. He was scholarly, with a wit at once broad and pedantic, and sometimes the two misunderstood each other. Gradually, they toned down the flirtatiousness of their correspondence, and although they exchanged letters at long intervals into the 1810s, the heady days of Paris were behind them.

In February of 1787, Congress granted Jefferson a leave of absence so that he could travel for his health, visiting spas to tend to his ailing wrists. His tour took him through southern France, with a detour to Italy, where he visited rice fields and pocketed samples that he shipped home in his diplomatic pouch to evade local laws against exporting rice. Riding in a modest carriage with one servant, he enjoyed his ability to travel anonymously. Surveying the countryside, he studied the lives of peasants and the state of agriculture, and saw as many Roman ruins as he could.

On March 20, 1787, he happily reported that he had finally beheld in person the Maison Carrée, a Roman structure located in the French city of Nîmes: "Here I am, Madam, gazing whole hours at the Maison quarrée, like a lover at his mistress. The stocking weavers and silk spinners around it, consider me as a hypochondriac Englishman, about to write with a pistol, the last chapter of his history." This building, one of his favorites, had inspired his design for the new Virginia capitol at Richmond even before he left Virginia

This 1786 letter from Jefferson to Maria Cosway dramatized the dialogue between his "head" and his "heart" about his conflicting feelings following Maria's departure from Paris. Written with his left hand because he had broken his right wrist in a fall, it was the longest letter Jefferson ever wrote.

for Europe; now he took great pains to commission an exact model of the Roman building to be shipped home to Virginia to guide the builders in Richmond.

Jefferson developed firm views about what Americans should and should not glean from the Old World. In a 1788 memorandum for two young Americans, Edward Rutledge of South Carolina and William Shippen of Pennsylvania, who sought his guidance for their travels, he urged them to study only those things that would be of use in America—agriculture, "mechanical arts," gardens, and architecture. He wrote that European politics were "well worth studying so far as respects internal affairs." Then he advised them to do as he had done:

> Examine their influence on the happiness of the people. Take every possible occasion for entering into the houses of the laborers, and especially at the moments of their repast; see what they eat, how they are clothed, whether they are obliged to work too hard; whether the government or their landlord takes from them an unjust proportion of their labor; on what footing stands the property they call their own, their personal liberty, &c., &c.

Most important, he warned his fellow citizens against paying too much attention to the courts of Europe, likening them to "the tower of London or menagerie of Versailles, with their lions, tigers, hyenas, and other beasts of prey, standing in the same relation to their fellows." And he bitterly quipped, "A slight acquaintance with them will suffice to show you that, under the most imposing exterior, they are the weakest and worst part of mankind." Later, he urged young Americans not to take the customary "Grand Tour" of Europe, because it was a swift and sure way to corrupt their habits and political sympathies.

The gap separating France's rich and poor appalled Jefferson. Noting how entrenched social differences damaged the people's virtue, industry, and happiness, he felt deep compassion for the rural poor. On one trip he met an old woman trudging by the side of the road, gave her a lift in his carriage, and questioned her about her life. When they reached her destination, he gave her a small sum of money, which turned out to be the equivalent of three days' wages for her, and she burst into tears. By contrast, Jefferson saw the urban poor not as fellow human beings deserving compassion but as the inevitable, degraded byproducts of cities. For the rest of his life, he begged his countrymen not "to pile upon one another in large cities," which he denounced as dens of wild beasts bent on eating one another.

Jefferson saw his travels in Europe as a crash course in the differences between the Old and New Worlds. Everywhere he looked, he saw corruption—rooted in monarchy, aristocracy, urbanization, and established churches—rotting European life. Unlike Europe, he insisted, America was growing happier, richer, and more virtuous almost daily.

In May 1787, soon after his return from his travels, Jefferson welcomed his eight-year-old daughter, Maria (nicknamed Polly), to Paris. Accompanying Polly was the slave Sally Hemings, then aged 14 (about Patsy's age). Sally was the daughter of Betty Hemings and John Wayles, and thus the half-sister of Jefferson's wife. Jefferson's in-laws chose her to travel with Polly because she already had experience taking care of Polly, who was deeply attached to her.

We have no portraits of Sally Hemings, but we know from later descriptions of her that she had a proud, erect bearing and was light-skinned, with long dark hair flowing down her back. We do not know whether she resembled Martha Wayles Jefferson. Jefferson's papers mention Sally Hemings only in matter-of-fact references to her as one among his nearly 200 slaves.

What we know of their relations during their time in Paris comes from the recollections of her son Madison Hemings (published in an Ohio newspaper in 1873) of her memories as told to him. Hemings recounted that in 1789, as Jefferson was preparing to return with his family to America, Sally, then 16, confronted him. She told him that she could stay in Paris as a free woman, taking advantage of French laws banning slavery, or she could return to Virginia as a slave. She exacted from Jefferson a promise that, if she returned to Virginia, he would free any children he fathered with her. There is no corroborating evidence whether Sally was pregnant by Jefferson in 1789, as Madison Hemings claims, or, if so, what happened to the child she was carrying.

While Jefferson was grappling with the new nation's diplomatic problems, fighting for America in the arena of ideas, wrestling with his conscience about slavery, and struggling with his feelings, he also confronted the challenges of being a single father. Soon after his arrival in Paris, he had enrolled Patsy in a convent school. He reassured Abigail Adams that the nuns had promised not to interfere with Patsy's religious views. When Polly arrived, he enrolled her in the same school to keep Patsy company and be guided by her example. They visited him two afternoons each week, spending the rest of the time at the convent. Meanwhile, he wrote them affectionate, demanding letters, listing what they should learn and how much time they should devote to study, drawing, knitting, needlepoint, and habits of personal cleanliness and dress.

By early 1788, Patsy was 15 years old, an age ripe for teenage rebellion. Either the nuns' religious fervor had won her over, or she chafed at their discipline and was hoping to persuade her father to remove her. Whatever the case, she wrote to Jefferson that she wanted to convert to Catholicism and become a nun. Immediately, he drove to the school, withdrew his daughters, and brought them back to live with him.

No matter how distracting his private concerns, Jefferson took his diplomatic duties seriously, and he kept an anxious eye on developments at home. Depending on friends for reliable news, he conducted an extensive correspondence that consumed each morning in writing and answering dozens of letters. As was customary in this period, he and his friends kept careful track of mail sent and received, which is why so many of Jefferson's letters begin by listing incoming and outgoing letters.

News of the American event that gave him greatest happiness arrived in a 1786 letter from James Madison. In 1785–86, Madison regularly reported on his efforts to resurrect the report of Jefferson's committee of law revisors. One of the first bills from that report that Madison rammed through the Virginia legislature was Jefferson's bill abolishing primogeniture.

At the same time, an unexpected controversy arose over a measure taking the opposite position from Jefferson's on church-state relations. Through the 1780s, two shifting coalitions competed for office and political power in Virginia. One group, more conservative in politics and religion, followed Patrick Henry; the other, more liberal group backed Jefferson, Madison, and George Mason. In 1785, in a bid for support from religious Virginians, Henry proposed a bill to use tax revenue to pay the salaries of Episcopalian and Presbyterian ministers; he hoped that this measure would woo the Presbyterians from the alliance backing Jefferson and Madison.

Henry's proposal backfired, however, embarrassing Presbyterians and angering Baptists and liberal Episcopalians. Petitions opposing Henry's bill flooded the legislature. One of them was James Madison's eloquent "Memorial and Remonstrance against Religious Assessments," which argued that separation of church and state was needed to protect the individual, the state, and religion from the corrupting alliance of church and state. Stunned by the public's angry reaction, the Virginia legislature defeated Henry's bill. Seizing his chance, Madison revived Jefferson's Bill for Religious Freedom. After dropping a few of its more radical clauses, the General Assembly enacted it into law.

Jefferson welcomed Madison's news with joy. He oversaw a translation of the Virginia Statute for Religious Freedom into French and had copies printed for distribution among his friends. Swiftly republished throughout Europe, the statute won Jefferson and Madison European fame, and it still stands as a landmark in the history of religious liberty.

Not all the news from America was as happy as the adoption of the Virginia Statute for Religious Freedom. In 1786, for example, debtors in western Massachusetts became furious at what they saw as the state legislature's indifference to their plight. An economic depression had combined with harsh British trade policies to squeeze anyone who owed money. British officials required Americans to pay all the debts they owed British creditors in gold and silver. This policy helped to set in motion a series of falling dominoes. Merchants in large cities demanded payment of debts from merchants in small towns, who, in turn, demanded payment from debtors such as farmers. When farmers could not pay, creditors sued, often seizing farmers' lands, houses, and personal property to satisfy the unpaid debts. Massachusetts farmers begged the legislature to put brakes on this process by suspending court sessions or by issuing new paper money to drive down the currency's value so that farmers could pay their debts more easily. The legislature refused, and in the summer of 1786 hundreds of farmers rose in revolt to save their homes.

The uprising took its name from Daniel Shays, a former captain of the Continental Army who became a symbol of rebellion, like Robin Hood in English folklore. Shays's Rebellion became a major crisis. One out of every four New England men old enough to bear arms took part in the uprising, which set off similar outbreaks as far south as Virginia and as far north as New Hampshire and Vermont. Finally, in January 1787, a force of more than 4,000 Massachusetts militiamen under the command of General Benjamin Lincoln defeated the rebels, and the rebellion collapsed.

News of the end of Shays's Rebellion did not reach Europe for months. Thus, when in early 1787 Jefferson got reports of the uprising, it was still raging, as far as he knew. He took the news calmly. He saw such rebellions as healthy signs of a spirited people defending liberty against even the best government on earth. On February 21, 1787, he wrote to Abigail Adams, "The spirit of resistance to government is so valuable on certain occasions, that I wish it to be always kept alive. It will often be exercised when wrong, but better so than not to be exercised at all. I like a little rebellion now and then. It is like a storm in the Atmosphere."

Writing on November 13, 1787, to William S. Smith (John and Abigail Adams' son-in-law) and on December 20, 1787, to James Madison, he used mathematics to explain why he was not alarmed by Shays's Rebellion. Deducing that one rebellion in one of thirteen states in ten years amounted to one rebellion in America in a century and a half, he told Madison, "No country should be so long without one." And, in his letter to Smith, he added, in words that have shocked later generations, "What signify a few lives lost in a century or two? The tree of liberty must from time to time be refreshed with the blood of patriots and tyrants. It is it's natural manure." Jefferson's reaction to Shays's Rebellion shows how, as an American abroad, he had come to idealize the United States, to paint the lives of Americans in rosy colors, and sometimes to let his eloquence carry him away.

While downplaying Shays's Rebellion and countering rumors that America was verging on collapse, Jefferson worried about the Confederation's real weaknesses, specifically its inability to pay even the interest on the nation's debts. Thus, he watched with hope the growing movement to revise or replace the Articles of Confederation, and welcomed the news that the Federal Convention was meeting in Philadelphia, perhaps to write a new constitution for the United States.

Besides its relevance to his diplomatic work, constitution-making fascinated Jefferson. In 1776, he had missed his chance to help create the Virginia constitution because he was representing Virginia in Congress. In *Notes on the State of Virginia,* he had harshly criticized that constitution, hoping to spur a movement for constitutional change in his native state. Now, as he got word of the Federal Convention, he realized that he was missing another experiment in government. Writing to John Adams on August 30, 1787, he showed a flash of envy:

> I have news from America as late as July 19. Nothing had then transpired from the Federal convention. I am sorry they began their deliberations by so abominable a precedent as that of tying up the tongues of their members. Nothing can justify this example but the innocence of their intentions, and ignorance of the value of public discussion. I have no doubt that all their other measures will be good and wise. It is really an assembly of demigods.

In November 1787, weeks after the Convention finished its work, Jefferson received printed copies of the proposed constitution from Washington, Franklin, and Madison. Studying it intently, he varied in his views of it, depending on whom he was writing to at the moment. On November 13, 1787, he told Adams,

> I confess there are things in it which stagger all my dispositions to subscribe to what such an assembly has proposed.... Indeed I think all the good of this new constitution might have been couched in three or four new articles to be added to the good, old, and venerable fabrick [the Articles of Confederation], which should have been preserved even as a religious relique.

To Madison, Jefferson wrote more hopefully. On December 20, 1787, he assured Madison that he admired the Constitution's system of checks and balances, under which any two branches of the federal government could restrain the third. He was "captivated" by the ways that the Constitution balanced the competing claims of large and small states, free and slave states, and the states and the federal government. He focused his criticism on two omissions: its lack of a bill of rights safeguarding individual liberty and its failure to limit the number of terms that the President could serve.

Jefferson predicted that future Presidential elections would pit an "Angloman" against a "Galloman" (a supporter of Britain against a supporter of France), and that both nations would try to corrupt the American political process. He also warned, "Experience concurs with reason in concluding that the first magistrate will always be re-elected if the Constitution permits it. He is then an officer for life."

On the issue of a bill of rights, Jefferson touched a vital nerve in the argument over the Constitution. In 1776, Virginians had invented the idea of a declaration of rights at the head of a written constitution, an innovation widely copied by the other states. The purpose of a declaration of rights was to state basic principles of government—rights as "right things"—that citizens could use to assess the actions of their representatives. Americans cherished and Europeans admired these bills of rights. Thus, Jefferson was surprised and dismayed that the proposed Constitution of the United States lacked a bill of rights. Nor was he alone. On November 10, 1787, John Adams asked him, "What think you of a Declaration of Rights? Should not such a Thing have preceeded the Model?"

Many Americans echoed Jefferson's and Adams's concerns. The lack of a bill of rights became the strongest argument against the Constitution, giving its backers unending trouble. Madison and other supporters of the Constitution, who called themselves Federalists, insisted that a bill of rights was a "parchment barrier" that a determined majority could punch through; Alexander Hamilton argued in *The Federalist No. 84* that the Constitution was a catalogue of rights, and that a bill of rights was not needed because the Constitution gave the federal government no power to invade rights. These arguments persuaded nobody. The Constitution's opponents, whom the Federalists saddled with the name Anti-Federalists, and even some Federalists, such as Edmund Pendleton, worried that the federal government might have power to injure rights. Even if there was no danger to liberty, Jefferson lectured Madison on December 20, 1787, "a bill of rights is what the people are entitled to against every government on earth, general or particular, & what no just government should refuse, or rest on inference."

In late 1787 and 1788, Americans divided over the Constitution. The controversy raged in Congress; in state legislatures, polling places, and ratifying conventions; and in newspapers, coffeehouses, and taverns. Federalists insisted that the Constitution had to be adopted as it was; Anti-Federalists argued that it had to be amended before they would agree to it.

Anxious about the Constitution's fate, Jefferson was frustrated at how slowly news from home reached him; each letter he wrote or received took six to eight weeks to cross the Atlantic. The delays, and the differing ideas that occurred to him from week to week, soon got him in trouble. In early 1788, he wrote to several correspondents that he hoped that nine states would adopt the Constitution, to give the United States a government that could deal with national problems. He also hoped, however, that the remaining states would refuse to ratify the Constitution until it was amended by the addition of a bill of rights.

Jefferson's idea had two flaws. The first was a matter of timing. His letters arrived in America after the Massachusetts ratifying convention, the sixth to adopt the Constitution, had endorsed a proposal made by leading Anti-Federalists Samuel Adams and John Hancock and accepted by William Cushing and his Federalist allies. The convention ratified the Constitution and adopted a list of amendments to be recommended to the first Congress to meet once the Constitution was ratified. The Federalists vowed to support these recommended amendments, and the Anti-Federalists agreed to accept the Constitution. This proposal cut through the stalemate of "ratify it as it is" versus "amend it before ratifying it." Every state but Maryland followed the Massachusetts plan, which Jefferson embraced once he heard about it.

The second flaw was more embarrassing. Problems posed by conducting politics through the mail plagued Jefferson and his contemporaries. He saw most of his letters as private, crafted only for the person to whom he wrote, not to be handed around or, worse yet, printed in newspapers. When he wrote to trusted friends such as Madison, he used a code of his own devising, so that only the letter's recipient could know what it meant. However, he was not consistent in this practice, often pouring out his ideas in highly quotable words to people who were careless of his privacy. Some of his correspondents published his letters, and Anti-Federalists and Federalists squabbled over whether he opposed or supported the Constitution.

When news of this controversy reached Jefferson, he was horrified. Having hoped only to give helpful advice, he was now the focus of a partisan brawl. Because he was 3,000 miles and two months away from the struggle, he had no way to set matters straight. It did not help that his closest friends were divided: Monroe opposed the Constitution and Madison supported it.

Nonetheless, Jefferson continued to urge Madison to support a bill of rights. At first, Madison resisted, repeating his argument that bills of rights were only "parchment barriers." Also, he wrote that, due to haste, forgetfulness, or sloppy draftsmanship, constitution-makers might leave rights out or not give them enough protection. Unpersuaded, Jefferson insisted that a bill of rights could do no harm and much good. As he assured Madison on March 15, 1789, "half a loaf is better than no bread. If we cannot secure all our rights, let us secure what we can." Jefferson helped to move Madison from a position of skepticism about written declarations of rights to one of cautious support of such amendments, and influenced the arguments that Madison made in the 1st Congress to support amending the Constitution.

Jefferson proved prophetic about another use for a bill of rights. As he wrote to Madison in the same letter,

> In the arguments in favor of a declaration of rights, you omit one which has great weight with me, the legal check which it puts into the hands of the judiciary. This is a body, which if rendered independent & kept strictly to their own department merits great confidence for their learning & integrity.

Here Jefferson was arguing for the theory of judicial review, in which a court interpreting a constitution has the power to strike down laws or executive actions as unconstitutional. Decisions by the U.S. Supreme Court declaring government actions limiting individual rights to be unconstitutional bear out his suggestion. Ironically, during and after his Presidency, when he faced a hostile federal judiciary led by Chief Justice John Marshall, Jefferson was more suspicious of "legal checks... [in] the hands of the judiciary."

The challenge of constitution-making, the contrast between Europe's corruption and misery and America's virtue and happiness, and the stirring early events of the French Revolution spurred Jefferson to ponder the proper relations between past and present, and between generations. On September 6, 1789, he wrote a letter to Madison that, he admitted, was pure speculation. Proposing the theme "The earth should belong... always to the living generation," he argued that no generation ought to be bound by the acts of those coming before it, and that in turn no generation ought to be able to bind those coming afterward. Yet again, he started to calculate, concluding that a generation's average life span was 19 years. Because of this fact, he reasoned, all forms of government, laws, and debts should expire every 19 years, leaving each generation free to establish its own government and laws and to contract its own debts. His aim in making this argument was to reinforce the contrast between an America free of inherited debts and a Europe tormented by them.

Writing in response from New York, where he was helping to launch the government under the Constitution, Madison pointed out that generations benefited from the labors of those who came before them, as in the cases of roads and bridges. Also, he noted, generations undertook projects that would benefit those who came after them. Madison concluded that just as benefits linked generations, so too should the burdens of paying for those benefits. He noted other flaws in Jefferson's theories, including the problem that generations did not succeed one another neatly every 19 years, and Jefferson conceded many of his points. Even so, for the rest of his life, Jefferson often returned to the linked themes of freedom, fresh starts, and the folly of old customs and laws binding new generations, reviving his beloved idea over and over again for a series of correspondents.

The open corruption and hidden weaknesses of French society, and Jefferson's anxiety to warn America against similar errors, spurred his speculations on generations. Like most Americans, however, he believed that things would continue in France as they had done. In his confidential reports to John Jay, he spelled out the problems of America's chief ally. He painted King Louis XVI as too young, weak, and stupid for his office, and he denounced Austrian-born Queen Marie Antoinette as vain, selfish, and out of touch with the people.

For months, Louis XVI had hired and fired one finance minister after another. Each realized what steps were needed to solve the nation's fiscal crisis: abolishing taxes that unfairly burdened the king's poorest subjects and imposing taxes on the nobles' estates and income. When each finance minister made these proposals, the nobility and the church united against such vital steps, the minister lost his job, and popular anger at the stalemate grew. Protests and outbreaks of rioting flared in Paris and in the countryside.

In 1788, despite protests from the queen and her conservative allies among the nobility, Louis XVI bowed to the inevitable. Under pressure from Lafayette and other liberal thinkers, he called elections to the Estates General, a special French representative assembly that had last met in 1634; on May 5, 1789, the Estates General convened, with Jefferson watching from the gallery. The Estates General had three equal chambers, for the three Estates, or layers of society: the clergy (first), the nobility (second), and the people (third).

In its last meetings in the 17th century, the First and Second Estates had voted down any proposal backed by the Third. This time, however, the people's representatives were having none of it. They insisted, in the words of the liberal clergyman Abbé Sieyès, that the Third Estate represented the whole nation, not just one-third of it. On June 17, 1789, the Third Estate declared itself the National Assembly. So the stalemate persisted, monitored by Jefferson. However, even he was unprepared for what followed.

Resenting the National Assembly, the church and the nobles talked the king into shutting it down. On the morning of June 20, 1789, the delegates of the Third Estate came to the chamber where the Estates General was meeting, only to discover that they had been locked out. Infuriated, they took over an unused indoor tennis court, convened as the National Assembly, and swore an oath (soon dubbed the "Tennis Court Oath") not to dissolve until their demands were met. Their defiance captured the people's imagination, and, on June 27, Louis XVI capitulated and legalized the National Assembly.

The queen and her allies among the aristocracy refused to give in. On July 11, they persuaded Louis XVI to dismiss his latest finance minister, the Swiss-born Jacques Necker. Necker had done no more to solve the fiscal crisis than his predecessors had, but the people saw him as a victim of the selfish clergy and nobility. On July 14, 1789, riots broke out in several districts of Paris. The rioters were infuriated that their needs—specifically, for bread—were being ignored and that the government was unable or unwilling to help them.

Each crowd raided a different Paris gatehouse, where customs officials collected taxes on grain convoys entering the city. A young lawyer, Camille Desmoulins, leaped onto a table at an outdoor café and urged the large surrounding crowd to take action. Shouting their approval, they marched on the Bastille, the vast ancient fortress used by generations of French monarchs as a prison but which was now an armory. Word of mouth spread the plan to the other rioters, who also

On July 14, 1789, several mobs of Parisians converged on and captured the Bastille. Jefferson, then American minister to France, was taken by surprise by the Bastille's fall, but embraced the cause of the French Revolution, which the fall of the Bastille launched.

marched on the Bastille. Joining forces, they stormed the Bastille, killing the guards defending it and the prison's governor, tearing his body apart in rage. Later the Bastille was demolished, under the orders of the Marquis de Lafayette, who was a favorite of the people and the politicians who claimed to speak for them. Lafayette asked Thomas Paine, the author of *Common Sense* and a fierce advocate of democratic revolution, to convey the Bastille's key to George Washington. (To this day, it hangs in a special case at Washington's home, Mount Vernon.)

The crisis brought into sharp relief the problems plaguing France. Once Louis XVI had been forced to embrace the National Assembly and had abandoned Versailles for the Tuileries Palace in Paris, the Assembly began to turn France into a constitutional monarchy, in which the king was bound by the rule of law. Liberal nobles and clergymen joined the National Assembly, making emotional shows of their commitment to the cause; on August 4, 1789, the National Assembly abolished the entire structure of French society, doing away with the separate three Estates. No longer would nobles or the clergy have special rights and privileges beyond those of ordinary people; everyone would be a citizen of France.

As they struggled to reform the French government, Lafayette and his allies begged Jefferson for advice. The Virginian was a diplomat from a foreign nation, which meant that he was supposed to stay neutral and not interfere in his host country's domestic affairs; repeatedly, Jefferson assured authorities in France and the United States that he was not violating his duty. However, his papers and those of the leaders who met at his home in Paris show that he played a more active role than he was willing to admit. For example, Jefferson contributed significantly to the drafting of the most famous document of the French Revolution, the Declaration of the Rights of Man and the Citizen, which the National Assembly proclaimed on August 26, 1789.

In Jefferson's view, the French were following paths that the American Revolution had marked out. Delighted that the French were trying to launch a constitutional monarchy and trying to learn from the American experience, he hoped that France would light the way for other European nations, perhaps even for Britain. Thomas Paine, who shuttled between Britain and France, shared Jefferson's hopes for an age of worldwide democratic revolution.

And yet there were ominous signs of the potential for violence and mayhem lurking beneath the happy surface of events. In April 1789, in an event known as the Réveillon Riots, the army opened fire on an angry Paris mob; Jefferson did not witness this event, but his cool report to John Jay endorsed the army's harsh measures, showing a lack of sympathy for the Parisian poor and a failure to grasp that the poor had the power to seize control of events in the capital.

By September 1789, Jefferson was making nervous, joking references to bloodthirsty mobs cutting off people's heads, and he installed bars on the windows of his house in response to the growing crime problem. Even so, he remained optimistic about events in France. That month, Jefferson finally received Congress's permission for another leave of absence, a request he had filed in November 1788, after negotiating the Consular Convention. He wanted to bring his daughters home to Virginia and to put his shaky finances in order, but he still hoped and planned to return to France as American minister. As it turned out, when he left Paris at the end of September 1789, he was leaving for good—though he did not know it yet.

On June 17, 1785, Jefferson had urged Monroe to visit Europe:

> The pleasure of the trip will be less than you expect but the utility greater. It will make you adore your own country, it's soil, it's climate, it's equality, liberty, laws, people & manners. My God! how little do my country men know what precious blessings they are in possession of,

and which no other people on earth enjoy. I confess I had no idea of it myself. . . .

This revealing letter shows how much Jefferson's exposure to Europe had affected him. Everywhere he went, he saw the blighting, corrupting effects of monarchy and aristocracy. He saw those evils in the hardness of a peasant's bed, in the condition of rutted roads, in the squalor and danger of city life. Before visiting Europe, he had never seen a city larger than Philadelphia, which in the early 1780s boasted a population of some 3,000. In comparison, Paris and London were behemoths, with hundreds of thousands of inhabitants and the full range of urban problems that revolted him and ever afterward made him a foe of cities.

Jefferson's observations of Europe, the growing dismay he felt, and the conclusions he reached about the Old World, shaped him for decades. They echo in his writings in the 1790s about the spirit of monarchy and aristocracy that he thought he saw warping American politics. They influenced the vehemence with which he defended the French Revolution long after most of his countrymen had given up on it. And they help to explain his almost fanatical devotion to republicanism and equality, and his hostility to those whom he saw as enemies of liberty and republican government. As Jefferson prepared to return home at the end of 1789, he brought with him a strong commitment to a coherent worldview—an ideology, in his word—that, ever afterward, shaped his vision of the world and his place in it. Ironically, Jefferson also brought home with him the underside of that ideology. In this way, Thomas Jefferson was his own best illustration of the dangers of an American spending time in Europe. Along with his new tastes for such luxuries as expensive books and fine European wines, the fears and suspicions he developed there haunted him for the rest of his life.

"THE PARTIES STYLED REPUBLICAN AND FEDERAL" (1789–1793)

On November 23, 1789, Thomas Jefferson, his family, and the servants and slaves who had been with them in France arrived in Norfolk, Virginia. Though Jefferson had planned to stay home for only six months, a letter from President George Washington greeted him on his arrival, informing him that he had been nominated and confirmed as the country's first secretary of state. When Washington pressed him to accept the post, he consented.

Much had changed in the United States since 1784, when Jefferson had sailed to France. The crisis of the Union in the mid-1780s, followed by the struggles to frame and adopt the Constitution, had transformed American politics and government. After the Confederation Congress declared the Constitution to be in effect, it launched the process of transition from government under the Articles of Confederation to government under the Constitution. By April of 1789, George Washington had been elected unanimously as the first President of the United States, the First Federal Congress had convened in New York City, and the nation was watching anxiously as its new government began its operations.

FEDERAL HALL.
Inauguration of Genl George Washington, the First President of the United States, on the 30.th of April 1789.

In 1789, George Washington was sworn in as the first President on the balcony of Federal Hall in New York City. Later that year, he persuaded Jefferson to become the first secretary of state.

Secretary of State Jefferson had to help direct the nation's course in world affairs, a task complicated by growing conflict over the French Revolution. As a member of Washington's cabinet, he also took part in its deliberations on domestic affairs. On both sets of issues, he clashed increasingly with Secretary of the Treasury Alexander Hamilton. Because the split between them shaped and reflected larger conflicts in American politics, setting former allies at odds with one another, Jefferson also played a vital part in the rise of strife between what he later called "the parties styled republican and federal."

Launching the government under the Constitution was a demanding process that enlisted the talents of the nation's leading figures, including Thomas Jefferson and John Adams. Both men found it difficult to reenter American public life after diplomatic service abroad. They had spent years dealing with monarchs and nobles, courts and salons, challenges far different from those they had known in their own country. Their difficulties took different forms, however.

Adams once had distrusted Europe and its aristocratic habits. Now he was convinced that titles and distinctions were needed to strengthen government, in the Old World and the New World alike. The Vice President was painfully unsure of himself, however, because the Constitution's framers had created his office almost as an afterthought. He tried to confirm his authority as president of the Senate by expounding parliamentary customs and classical precedents, but his insistence on doing so, and his losing campaign to give the President a grand title, made him a laughingstock.

Jefferson's diplomatic experience, on the other hand, had taught him to stress differences between the Old World and the New World. His memories of the gap separating rich and poor in France and of the corruption of France's government fixed in his mind an idealized picture of life in America and a horrific image of what he hoped America would never become. He was enthralled by the French Revolution's hopeful beginning, in which liberal aristocrats—people like himself—embraced democracy, rejecting titles and customs of monarchy and aristocracy, leading the people to liberty. He came home determined to advance that noble cause.

Jefferson delayed his departure from Monticello to host the wedding of his 17-year-old daughter, Martha (Patsy), to Thomas Mann Randolph. Thus, he did not arrive in New York, the nation's temporary capital, to take up his duties as secretary of state until March 21, 1790. What he found there challenged his vision of America. No longer could he believe that all Americans were honest farmers resisting corruption. In New York, or so he recalled as an old man, he found scenes of despair. To his disbelieving eyes, Americans seemed to be aping the aristocratic habits of Europe; to his horrified ears came what he thought was praise of kingly government. In his view, the danger was clear. Corruption had taken root. Americans eager to create a nation had embraced the wrong model for its politics, that of monarchy. The victims of this wrong turn would be the Revolution's achievements and the people's liberties.

New York was an anxious city. For politicians nervous about taking part in an experiment in government, a major test was how to present oneself. A politician who wanted to be seen as a leader had to display himself to the people as worthy of their trust. He could not indulge in too much luxury—overly fine clothing, too many horses to draw his carriage—or he risked being dismissed as arrogant and hostile to republican government. Descriptions of Jefferson from this time suggest that he dressed and carried himself to present a silent, critical commentary on what he felt were the new nation's aristocratic manners.

For example, on May 24, 1790, Jefferson appeared before a Senate committee to testify on salaries for American diplomats. One senator on the committee, William Maclay of Pennsylvania, found the capital's high-toned manners as dismaying as Jefferson did. In his diary, Maclay recorded his impressions of men and manners; all the government's major figures passed under his scrutiny. Few of them made a favorable impression on him, including Jefferson. Maclay noted that Jefferson "has rather the air of stiffness in his manners," that "his clothes seem too small for him," and that he slouched in his seat. He continued:

> He had a rambling, vacant look, and nothing of that firm, collected deportment which I expected would dignify the presence of a secretary or minister. I looked for gravity, but a laxity of manner seemed shed about him. He spoke almost without ceasing. But even his discourse

partook of his personal demeanor. It was loose and rambling, and yet he scattered information wherever he went, and some even brilliant sentiments sparkled from him. . . .

Maclay's sketch clashes with the portraits of Jefferson by the French sculptor Jean Antoine Houdon and the American painter Charles Willson Peale. Houdon's bust, one of the finest likenesses of Jefferson ever made, shows the Virginian faultlessly attired, with his head held high, conveying personal and intellectual confidence. Peale's portrait also shows a confident man of middle age, carefully yet simply dressed and coiffed, his most arresting features being his red hair and piercing hazel eyes.

Jefferson needed all the confidence he could muster, for his office was an untried part of a new system of government. Although in theory he was the nation's chief diplomat, he found that President Washington was resolved to be his own secretary of state, though he often sought Jefferson's advice. Congress assigned the State Department other tasks, such as running the post office, granting patents to inventors, and establishing federal standards of coinage, weights, and measures. This last mandate appealed to Jefferson's scientific interests; on July 13, 1790, he sent Congress a report on the subject that became one of his most important state papers. Congress adopted his proposal of decimal coinage (one dollar = one hundred cents) but rejected his idea for devising a system of weights and measures resembling the metric system later adopted in France.

Washington regularly consulted Chief Justice John Jay and leading members of Congress, particularly Representative James Madison. His key advisors in the executive branch, with whom he conferred regularly in what we now call "cabinet meetings," were the heads of the State, Treasury, and War Departments, and the attorney general (the Justice Department was not created until 1870): Secretary of State Thomas Jefferson, Secretary of the Treasury Alexander Hamilton, Secretary of War Henry Knox, and

Attorney General Edmund Randolph. The cabinet's ablest members were Jefferson and Hamilton, two men notably different in physique, character, oratory, and philosophy. And Hamilton had lost no time in establishing himself as the President's most trusted advisor.

Hamilton was younger than Jefferson by more than a decade. Born in 1755 in the West Indies, an illegitimate child of a Scottish father and a French mother, he used his remarkable talents and abilities to rise from poverty and obscurity. While a student at King's College (now Columbia University), he threw himself into the Revolution's pamphlet war on the American side. When anti-Loyalist riots closed the college before he could finish his degree, Hamilton used his savings to organize the First New York Company of Artillery, with himself as captain.

In January 1777, impressed by Hamilton's efficiency, Washington named him an aide-de-camp with the rank of lieutenant colonel. For four years, he was indispensable to Washington in running the war. In February 1781, the two had a falling-out and Hamilton resigned from Washington's staff; but that October, at the pivotal battle of Yorktown, Washington gave him a field command and he distinguished himself for valor.

On leaving the army in 1782, Hamilton qualified for the New York bar and was named a New York delegate to the Confederation Congress. Energetic, direct, and occasionally tactless, throughout the 1780s he was a leading advocate of national constitutional reform. In the ratification controversy of 1787–88, besides helping to lead New York's Federalists, he planned *The Federalist,* a series of newspaper essays that he wrote with Madison and Jay. Washington named him secretary of the treasury, but only after more seasoned candidates, such as Senator Robert Morris of Pennsylvania, had turned down the job.

At first, Hamilton and Jefferson worked cordially together. They agreed that the nation's worst problem was its staggering

Jefferson's foremost opponent, Alexander Hamilton, was the nation's first and greatest secretary of the treasury and a leading advocate of broad interpretation of the Constitution.

burden of debt, which was of two types: debts owed by the United States and debts owed by the states for money borrowed from creditors at home and abroad. The federal government was responsible for the Confederation's debts, but although some states had repaid most or all of their debts, others had done nothing at all. These state debts were a source of continuing controversy among the states and a source of unending problems for American officials negotiating with foreign powers.

In his first "Report on the Public Credit," which he sent to Congress on January 14, 1790, Hamilton laid out the first part of his solution. The federal government would take over the states' debts, consolidate them with the federal debts, and issue securities—formal documents, such as savings bonds, that could substitute for hard cash. The proceeds from sales of these securities would gradually pay off part of the amassed national debt; the rest, represented by securities circulating in the economy, would support the nation's currency and help spur economic growth.

That spring, Congress deadlocked over the Funding Bill based on Hamilton's report. As Jefferson recalled, he was walking near the President's house when he ran into Hamilton. Haggard and distraught, Hamilton "walked me backwards and forward before the president's door for half an hour," explaining how the bill's failure would endanger the nation's credit at home and abroad, perhaps jeopardizing the Union.

These points had great weight with Jefferson, who recalled the problems that American debts had caused him during his diplomatic service. He offered to host a dinner at which he, Hamilton, and Madison (the bill's chief opponent) could hammer out a compromise. At that dinner, Madison agreed to end his active opposition to the Funding Bill and to release enough votes to win it a majority in the House. In exchange, Hamilton agreed to endorse a site for the permanent national capital along the Potomac River between Virginia and Maryland, a plan dear to the hearts of Virginians such as Jefferson, Madison, and Washington. The government would relocate to Philadelphia in late 1790, and would move to its permanent home in 1800.

Why was the permanent capital so controversial? And why did Madison and Jefferson deem its site a prize worth conceding the Funding Bill? From the nation's beginnings, the Continental and Confederation Congresses had moved from city to city, dramatizing the government's weakness and embarrassing American officials at home and in Europe. Seeking stability, the Federal Convention wrote into the Constitution a clause giving the federal government a permanent home in a district "ten miles square," but the Constitution did not say where that district would be. In 1788, once the Constitution was ratified, the Confederation Congress wasted more than two months in bitter, inconclusive debate on the capital issue. On October 10, Congress gave up; the new government would begin in New York, which had hosted Congress since 1784.

During 1789–90, the struggle for the permanent capital seethed beneath the surface of national politics. Much was at stake in choosing the site: not only the value of land investments and the business the capital would bring to the lucky city, but also deeper issues of politics and national character. If the capital were an existing city, such as Philadelphia, commercial and financial interests, dominant in New England, New York, and Pennsylvania, would have greatest weight in shaping national policy and defining national character. If the capital were a new city in a rural area, agricultural interests, dominant in the southern states, would exert the strongest influence. The dispute over the permanent capital therefore was also a sectional crisis, the first the Union faced under the Constitution. Recognizing this danger, Jefferson thought that a rural capital would protect the people's virtue and preserve republican government. For this reason, when Hamilton agreed to a capital on the Potomac, Jefferson thought that he had helped achieve the best result.

After the enactment of the law creating the Federal City, Jefferson worked with the French-born Major Pierre Charles L'Enfant, whom Washington had named to lay out the capital. To aid L'Enfant, Jefferson chose Benjamin Banneker, an ex-slave and self-taught mathematician. Banneker had challenged Jefferson's racial theories in *Notes on the State of Virginia;* to prove his abilities, he sent Jefferson a copy of his almanac, based on rigorous calculations of the times for the rising and setting of the sun and the moon, the phases of the moon, eclipses, and tide tables. On August 30, 1791, Jefferson answered:

[N]o body wishes more than I do to see such proofs as you exhibit, that nature has given to our black brethren talents equal to those of the other colours of men, & that the appearance of a want of them is owing merely to the degraded condition of their existence both in Africa and in America. I can add with truth that no body wishes more ardently to see a good system commenced for raising the condition both of their body & mind to what it ought to be, as fast as the imbecility of their present existence, and other circumstances which cannot be neglected, will admit.

In October 1809, however, Jefferson wrote to his friend, the poet and traveler Joel Barlow, that he suspected that Banneker had had help in preparing his almanac.

The summer of 1790 brought the first difference between Jefferson and Hamilton. Spain seized four British ships in Canada's Nootka Sound, claiming that they had violated Spanish territory. War between the two powers would make their colonies zones of battle, threatening American interests. When Britain and Spain appealed to the United States, Jefferson hoped to win concessions on trade and territory from both powers. Backed by Washington and Jefferson, Hamilton met with a private emissary from Britain, Major George Beckwith. But Hamilton went beyond his mandate, hinting to Beckwith that he would step in should Jefferson take too harsh a stance toward Britain, and he kept his remarks from the President and the secretary of state. That fall, having failed to win French support, Spain released the British ships, and the two nations agreed that each had a right to land on territory not yet claimed by any nation.

Domestic policy raised the first open breach between the two men. In February 1791, Congress passed a bill creating the Bank of the United States. A keystone of Hamilton's program, as set forth in his 1790 "Report on a National Bank," the Bank would be the central institution of the American economy. It would administer the consolidated American debts, issue securities for investors to purchase, regulate trade in them, and monitor the value of the nation's currency. Because the Constitution does not give the federal government specific power to create a bank, Washington asked his cabinet whether he should sign the bill. Jefferson and Randolph insisted that the Constitution gave the government only powers it specified and only those added powers necessary to exercise its specified powers. As the Bank was neither authorized by the Constitution nor necessary to any power under the Constitution, the bill was unconstitutional, and Washington should veto it.

Troubled, Washington asked Hamilton to answer Randolph's and Jefferson's opinions; he also asked Madison to draft a veto message. In a single day, Hamilton penned a long, brilliant memorandum. Like Jefferson and Randolph, he stressed the Constitution's clause giving Congress all powers "necessary and proper" to carry out its specific powers and duties, but he argued that "necessary" meant "useful" or "well suited." If a power achieves a goal specified in the Constitution or helps to exercise another granted power, and it is not banned by the Constitution, it is constitutional. Hamilton then showed that the Bank would help achieve many goals set forth in the Constitution and that nothing in the document prohibited it. Convinced by Hamilton, Washington signed the bill into law. The argument between Hamilton and Jefferson about interpreting the Constitution has raged from their time to our own; their memos remain the most influential statements of "strict" and "broad" constructions of the Constitution.

Afterward, Jefferson and Hamilton clashed more often and more bitterly. Even their personal traits set them apart. Hamilton, relatively short and slight, had the ramrod-straight posture of a former artillery officer; the lanky Jefferson tended to slouch (according to Maclay). Hamilton, a skilled orator, spoke with vehemence and passion; Jefferson, a poor speaker, disliked addressing an audience. Hamilton was abrupt, tactless, and combative; Jefferson was quiet, indirect, and diplomatic. Finally, Hamilton, who had risen from poverty by his own talent and energy, distrusted the people; Jefferson, a Virginia aristocrat from birth, hailed the people as the source of virtue and wisdom. Each man had a different vision of what sort of government the nation needed, and each loathed the other's vision as much as he prized his own. They agreed that the Constitution was an experiment in government whose success or failure would decide whether human beings could govern themselves, and they agreed that the experiment's outcome was in doubt. But these points of agreement increased the urgency of the question: Whose vision of America would prevail?

Jefferson feared that Hamilton had plans radically at odds with the Constitution. As he saw it, Hamilton wanted to warp the federal government out of constitutional shape, converting it into a copy of the British government, built on debt, corruption, and influence. Hamilton's goal, Jefferson charged, was to ally the rich and well born with the government at the people's expense, creating a corrupt aristocracy and destroying the virtue that was the basis of republican government.

Only a republic could preserve liberty, Jefferson insisted, and only virtue among the people could preserve a republic. And agriculture, he contended, was the true basis of republican virtue. As he had written in *Notes on the State of Virginia,* "Those who labor in the earth are the chosen people of God, if ever He had a chosen people, whose breasts he has made his peculiar deposit for substantial and genuine virtue." To preserve liberty, Jefferson argued, government had to be as close to the people as possible. To him, that meant a decentralized government, giving power over domestic issues to the states, the level of government closest to the people, and not to a distant federal government.

In contrast, Hamilton saw himself as free from local interests and prejudices, a true advocate of the national interest. Rejecting the claim that he was biased against agriculture, he argued for a balanced economy resting on agriculture, commerce, and manufacturing, with each supporting the other two. Doubting that the state governments could respond to national problems, he maintained that only a strong general government could defend American interests effectively. Finally, he did not share Jefferson's faith in the people's wisdom, nor did he believe that allying the rich with the government would create a corrupt aristocracy and destroy liberty.

The role of the United States in world affairs also set Jefferson and Hamilton at odds. The Western world was split into two blocs, one led by Britain and the other by France. Jefferson urged the nation to side with France and against Britain, because commerce and speculation had corrupted Britain, destroying British liberty. Also, he warned, the British, still hostile to America, were devising schemes to hamper American commerce. Jefferson feared that Hamilton's policies would enslave the United States to the dangerous, corrupt nation from which Americans had won their independence. Further, he insisted, gratitude and shared values required the United States to remain loyal to France, for French arms and loans had played vital roles in winning American independence. Finally, he argued that the ideals of the French Revolution—liberty and equality—were the ideals of the American Revolution. By standing against the French Revolution, Jefferson declared, Britain was an enemy not just of the United States but of the hopes of the world.

By contrast, Hamilton maintained that his fiscal program would foster a strong economy that would make the new nation worthy of respect on the world stage. He stressed that Britain, the world's leading naval power, had the greatest ability to hobble American trade and to attack American territory. Like other Federalists, Hamilton distrusted the French Revolution, fearing that it might unleash social forces that could destroy religion, morality, and good order. For these reasons, Hamilton urged the United States to remain neutral and rethink its alliance with a nation whose government seemed to symbolize anarchy and murder.

Once the French Revolution became a defining issue in America, Jefferson became a symbol of that conflict. Though hoping to avoid controversy, he voiced his views freely in private, only to experience profound embarrassment when they became public. In 1791, for example, he wrote a private letter to J. B. Smith, Thomas Paine's publisher, hailing *Rights of Man,* Paine's defense of the Revolution, as a counter to "the political heresies which have sprung up among us"; but he was appalled when Smith printed this letter, without his consent, as the preface to the American edition of Paine's book.

Long after many Americans recoiled from the French Revolution, Jefferson defended it, excusing what others saw as its atrocities: mob violence, massacres, and mass executions, often by the new-fangled machine known as the guillotine. On January 3, 1793, he scolded his friend and protégé William Short for denouncing the Revolution, even though Short had seen these terrible events firsthand. Jefferson declared the Revolution "necessary," although "many guilty persons fell without the forms of trial, and with them some innocent." He likened those innocent deaths to battlefield casualties:

> It was necessary to use the arm of the people, a machine not quite so blind as balls and bombs, but blind to a certain degree. . . . The liberty of the whole earth was depending on the issue of the contest, and was ever such a prize won with so little innocent blood? My own affections have been deeply wounded by some of the martyrs to this cause, but rather than it should have failed, I would have seen half the earth desolated. Were there but an Adam & an Eve left in every country, & left free, it would be better than as it is now.

Standing against those who stressed the innocent blood spilled by the French Revolution, Jefferson insisted that the costs in human misery that the old system had wrung from the French people far outweighed the costs of the revolution that swept the old system away.

In particular, the French Revolution helped to divide Jefferson from John Adams. In his controversial books *A Defence of the Constitutions of Government...* (1787–88) and *Discourses on Davila* (1790), Adams argued that some nations were better suited to self-government than others were. In his view, only a politically mature and experienced people, such as the Americans, who had governed themselves for nearly two centuries, could assume the blessings and responsibilities of free government.

The French, who had lived for centuries under a corrupt monarchy, lacked the knowledge and habits to make a republic work. By contrast, Jefferson insisted that all peoples had the right to govern themselves, no matter what their former governments were, and that they could, should, and someday would emulate the American Revolution. Jefferson's letter praising Paine's *Rights of Man* targeted Adams's *Discourses on Davila* as a key example of what Jefferson called the "heresies" of "monarchism," another reason why he was mortified when his letter was published, revealing his dispute with Adams to the world.

The divisions plaguing Washington's cabinet reflected and shaped those flaring in Congress and the nation. The Senate backed the administration, but the House was divided. Madison was increasingly moving into opposition, and his relations with President Washington were eroding. Hamilton's allies now spoke for the administration in the House. Struggling for alliances with like-minded members of Congress, Jefferson and Hamilton helped to spread partisan rancor throughout the government.

Thus, by the early 1790s, two groups of politicians were ranged against each other, disputing national policy at home and abroad. Calling themselves Federalists, backers of the Washington administration argued that they were the true heirs of the Constitution's supporters of 1787–88. Their foes, supporting Jefferson and Madison, took the name Republicans, insisting that they, not the Federalists, supported liberty and republican government. They made their case against the Federalist agenda in terms of political and social equality, advocating values that we think of as "democratic." Thus, even though in his private life, tastes, and habits, Jefferson was the model of an aristocratic Virginia gentleman, in the political realm he came to be seen, by friends and foes alike, as a symbol of democracy.

As the French Revolution convulsed France and then Europe, Jefferson's foes linked him with its excesses. They charged that he was as hostile to good order and religious institutions as the most radical French leaders, and that he wanted to unleash on the American people the madness tormenting France. At the same time, Jefferson's supporters hailed him as a fearless champion of the rights of the people and an unwavering foe of the corruption they associated with Hamilton's financial measures.

Where did Jefferson stand? He loathed Hamilton's policies, charging that they threatened to create a corrupt American aristocracy, which would erode American liberty and undermine republican government. And he went as far as his most radical supporters in seeing threats of monarchy and aristocracy in every line of Hamilton's fiscal program and administrative agenda. In particular, Jefferson's belief that the new nation had to remain a nation of farmers to preserve its virtue and liberty clashed with Hamilton's arguments, particularly in his 1791 "Report on Manufactures," that the United States had to encourage the growth of industry to compete with Britain and Europe in the world economy. But how democratic was he? Jefferson preserved a discreet silence on such questions, leaving his supporters free to believe what they wished. As he later told John Adams, he believed in "a natural aristocracy among men," grounded on "virtue and talent."

The point, however, is not what Jefferson believed, but what he symbolized in the eyes of his fellow citizens. They were convinced that he stood for an America in which all people have a voice in their nation's government, and in which no one would have special privileges based on birth or upbringing.

As the nation divided into Federalists and Republicans, each group called the other the worst name possible: "party." Most Americans feared the idea of party; believing that a society should unite to achieve the public good, they denounced parties as groups of ambitious men selfishly competing for power. Worse, parties were danger signals for a republic; if parties dominated a republic's politics, its days were numbered. The "parties" of the 1790s were not modern political parties—organized, disciplined groups of people who make politics their full-time profession and career. Rather, they were "partisan alliances"—shifting coalitions of politicians allied to pursue shared visions of what was best for the United States, and to oppose what they thought their foes stood for.

In this unstable political world, character and reputation were vital. Politicians stood or fell as leaders based on the public's view of their character and reputation. Thus, politicians eagerly, even desperately, sought information about one another. They were obsessed with political gossip, and Jefferson was a master of the game. He was deft at "collecting" public opinion and at helping to spread news of his opponents' words and deeds to undermine their standing. He would scribble reports, anecdotes, even rumors, filing them for his own reference. He believed that these memoranda would illuminate the murky world of the early Republic's politics, revealing the Federalists as dangerous advocates of monarchy and enemies of liberty and showing the Republicans as the saviors of their country.

One story, which Jefferson told to Benjamin Rush in 1811, described a dinner he had hosted for Adams and Hamilton. The conversation turned to the British constitution. Adams insisted that, purged of its corruption, it would be the most perfect form of government; Hamilton replied that its corruption was what made it work. Later, noticing three portraits framed on the wall, Hamilton asked Jefferson who they were. Jefferson named them as "my trinity of the three greatest men the world had ever produced": Lord Francis Bacon, the philosopher of science; Sir Isaac Newton, the scientist who had defined the laws of gravity; and John Locke, the philosopher of liberty and the human mind. As Jefferson recalled, Hamilton "paused for some time: 'the greatest man,' said he, 'that ever lived, was Julius Caesar.'" Some scholars insist that Jefferson rightly detected Hamilton's desire to become the American Caesar. Others argue that Hamilton was praising Caesar by Bacon's test of greatness— that the greatest men were founders of states and commonwealths, like Caesar. Still others suspect that Hamilton was indulging his mischievous sense of humor and goading the pedantic, humorless Jefferson.

In 1791, the year that Charles Willson Peale painted this portrait of Thomas Jefferson, the secretary of state was 48 years old and beginning his bitter struggle with Alexander Hamilton to determine the fate of the American constitutional experiment.

In these first years of the new government, agreeing in their opposition to Hamilton's program, Jefferson and Madison laid the groundwork for a new partisan alliance. In May 1791, while Congress was in recess, they toured the northern states. It was only a natural-history expedition, Jefferson insisted. However, while in New York, Hamilton's home state, the Virginians met with Hamilton's leading foes, Robert R. Livingston and Aaron Burr, hoping to form an alliance opposing Hamilton's policies. This alliance required a journalistic voice; Hamilton had a powerful ally in the *Gazette of the United States,* edited by John Fenno. Jefferson and Madison therefore decided to found a newspaper to counter Fenno's flood of pro-Hamilton propaganda. Madison's Princeton classmate, the poet and essayist Philip Freneau, agreed to move to Philadelphia to edit the *National Gazette.* To help Freneau make ends meet, Jefferson hired him as a part-time translator for the State Department.

The *National Gazette* pounded Hamilton. For example, the writer "Brutus" (a pen name taken from the Roman senator who slew Julius Caesar to save Roman liberty) charged,

> It does not appear to me to be a question of federalism or antifederalism, but it is the Treasury of the United States against the people.... The influence which the treasury has on our government is truly alarming; it already forms a center, around which our political system is beginning to revolve.

In unsigned essays for the *National Gazette,* written at Jefferson's urging, Madison insisted that the contest was between those devoted to republican liberty and those enslaved by aristocratic corruption. Other Republicans joined Madison, some of them, such as James Monroe and John Beckley (the clerk of the U.S. House of Representatives), also encouraged by Jefferson. Enraged by the *National Gazette's* attacks, and deducing that Jefferson and Madison were behind them, Hamilton responded with a stream of newspaper essays under a host of pen names, many of them targeting Jefferson, and other Federalists joined the fray.

As partisan division spread through the nation, the battle between Jefferson and Hamilton continued to rage in cabinet meetings. Convinced of the rightness of his views, Hamilton orated as though he were addressing Congress, aiming occasional barbs at Jefferson, who would simmer in frustration, sometimes making sardonic comments to take the wind out of Hamilton's sails.

Caught between his leading advisors, Washington suffered from their constant feuding. Not as quick-thinking as Hamilton or Jefferson, he preferred to ponder in private, taking time to reach decisions. Decades later, Jefferson recalled that

> [Washington's] mind was great and powerful, without being of the very first order; his penetration strong, though not so acute as that of a Newton, Bacon, or Locke; and as far as he saw, no judgment was ever sounder. It was slow in operation, being little aided by invention or imagination, but sure in conclusion.... Perhaps the strongest feature in his character was prudence, never acting until every circumstance, every consideration, was maturely weighed; refraining if ever he saw a doubt, but, when once decided, going through with his purpose, whatever obstacles opposed.

Washington had need of his judgment and his prudence, for it was only his advisors'—and the nation's—shared confidence in it and in him that held his government together.

But Washington was increasingly aware of the toll that age and illness were taking on him. Now sixty, he was haunted by the knowledge that no other male adult in his family had survived into his fifties; he saw himself as an old man who had lived beyond his time. Also, he was at least as thin-skinned as Jefferson was. Though he never publicly voiced frustration at criticism of his policies and himself, he exploded in wrath in the privacy of his cabinet. Most painful of all, Washington found the Presidency a thankless, terrifying burden. He fretted that every decision he made, every act and every failure to act, would set a precedent for future generations. He had assembled a group of advisors who, he hoped, would help him in leading the government. Instead, they brought him new problems and anxieties.

In the spring of 1792, weary of the infighting that threatened to tear his administration to pieces, Washington considered retiring at the end of his term. The prospect alarmed Hamilton and Jefferson. Insisting that his leadership was indispensable to the American experiment, both men argued that he had a duty to stay in office. On May 23, 1792, Jefferson wrote:

> The confidence of the whole union is centred in you. Your being at the helm, will be more than an answer to

every argument which can be used to alarm & lead the people in any quarter into violence or secession. North & South will hang together, if they have you to hang on....

Writing on July 30, Hamilton agreed: "[Y]our declining [a second term] would be deplored as the greatest evil, that could befall the country at the present juncture." Reluctantly heeding his advisors' views, Washington agreed to stand for a second term, which he won unanimously.

Although Hamilton and Jefferson had joined to persuade Washington to stay in office, their relations continued to worsen. That summer, the President appealed to them to end their bickering. On August 23, Washington wrote to Jefferson, "My earnest wish, and my fondest hope therefore is, that instead of wounding suspicions, and irritable charges, there may be liberal allowances—mutual forbearances—and temporising yieldings on all sides." He sent a nearly identical letter to Hamilton. On September 9, both men answered Washington by trading charges. Hamilton complained:

> I consider myself as the deeply injured party.... I know that I have been an object of uniform opposition from Mr. Jefferson, from the first moment of his coming to the City of New-York to enter upon his present office. I know, from the most authentic sources, that I have been the frequent subject of the most unkind whispers and insinuating from the same quarter. I have long seen a formed party in the Legislature, under his auspices, bent upon my subversion.

Even so, he declared his willingness to help find a peaceful solution to the impasse:

> I most sincerely regret the causes of the uneasy sensations you experience. It is my most anxious wish, as far as may depend upon me, to smooth the path of your administration, and to render it prosperous and happy. And if any prospect shall be open of healing or terminating the differences which exist, I shall most cheerfully embrace it....

By contrast, Jefferson wrote nothing that Washington could read as an olive branch. Exasperated by his treatment at Hamilton's hands, yearning to leave government to return to private life, and so angry that his words stumbled over themselves, he exploded in vexation, even aiming a touch of snobbery at Hamilton:

> To a thorough disregard of the honors & emoluments of office I join as great a value for the esteem of my countrymen, & conscious of having merited it by an integrity which cannot be reproached, & by an enthusiastic devotion to their rights & liberty, I will not suffer my retirement to be clouded by the slanders of a man whose history, from the moment at which history can stoop to notice him, is a tissue of machinations against the liberty of the country which has not only received and given him bread, but heaped it's honors on his head.

Jefferson saw himself as Hamilton's senior in age and public service, and expected that, as Virginians, he and Washington should see eye to eye, especially when confronting a New Yorker whose lowly origins could not match their own roots in Virginia's planter elite. Jefferson also believed that Hamilton had duped him into backing the Funding Bill and the Compromise of 1790. He now saw those measures as the basis of Hamilton's plan to turn the United States into a consolidated nation with a corrupt, aristocratic government. In his view, Hamilton was trying to cement a corrupt alliance between the government and commercial and speculating interests, based on policies designed to buy their loyalty and reward their support. Finally, he writhed under the sting of Hamilton's newspaper attacks. Jefferson insisted to Washington that, unlike Hamilton, he had never written a word for the newspapers attacking Hamilton. However, he did not admit that he had encouraged—even begged—others to do so.

On October 18, 1792, Washington tried to placate Jefferson, but at the same time he was frank about his unhappiness with the tumult plaguing his administration: "I regret, deeply regret," he wrote, "the differences in opinion which have arisen and divided you and another principal officer of the Government. I have a great, a sincere esteem for you both."

Washington's peacemaking efforts were in vain. By this point, Hamilton was convinced that Jefferson, Madison, and their allies in the House were seeking his destruction, and Jefferson was sure that Hamilton, leading a "corrupt squadron" of senators, representatives, and hack writers, was waging war on him in the press. In sum, each man had come to believe that the other was bent on driving him from the government, and responded in kind.

In early 1793, Virginians in the House tried to use Congress's power of investigation against Hamilton. Jefferson worked with them, drafting a set of resolutions attacking Hamilton's conduct of Treasury business and demanding a full inquiry. If the House adopted these resolutions, Jefferson hoped that its investigation of Hamilton would expose his corruption and force his resignation. Representative William Branch Giles of Virginia led the charge but toned down the resolutions before proposing them. The House rejected even this milder version, however, giving Hamilton another victory and Jefferson another rebuff.

Just as Jefferson was becoming the Republicans' symbolic national leader, he was wearying of the strains and struggles of politics. He had wanted to step down in 1792, at the end of Washington's first term, but he postponed his retirement several times, for he did not want to give the impression that Hamilton had driven him from the government. In September 1792, Hamilton learned of Jefferson's wish to retire; in a newspaper essay, he mocked Jefferson's claims to be "the quiet, modest, retiring philosopher," charging rather in an anonymous newspaper essay that he was "the intriguing incendiary, the aspiring turbulent competitor" who hoped to succeed Washington as President.

Jefferson's growing wish to leave politics worried his allies. On May 27, 1793, Madison warned, "[Y]ou must not make your final exit from public life till it will be marked with justifying circumstances which all good citizens will respect & to which your friends can appeal." In response, on June 9, Jefferson complained:

> To my fellow-citizens the debt of service has been fully & faithfully paid....I have now been in the public service four & twenty years; one half of which has been spent in total occupation with their affairs, & absence from my own. I have served my tour then.... The motion of my blood no longer keeps time with the tumult of the world. It leads me to seek for happiness in the lap and love of my family, in the society of my neighbors & my books, in the wholesome occupation of my farm & my affairs, in an interest or affection in every bud that opens, in every breath that blows around me, in an entire freedom of rest or motion..., owing account to myself alone of my hours & actions.... Indeed my dear friend, duty being out of the question, inclination cuts off all argument, & so never let there be more between you & me, on this subject.

At the end of July, Jefferson offered his resignation, but Washington persuaded him to delay it until year's end. That summer, American relations with France exploded in controversy, making Jefferson's last months in office among the most vexing of his career.

War had erupted between the Revolutionary French Republic and an alliance of monarchies led by Britain, Austria, and Prussia; the revolutionaries' execution of Louis XVI on January 21, 1793, embittered the conflict. Within the United States, violent political disagreement erupted over what the American response to these events should be. That spring, Washington and his advisors considered proclaiming that the nation would remain neutral. Jefferson opposed this step, arguing that only Congress had the power to declare the nation at peace, by analogy to its power to declare war. Realizing that he was outvoted, he backed Edmund Randolph's careful draft of the Neutrality Proclamation, and, on April 22, 1793, Washington issued the proclamation. Then Hamilton offered a written opinion arguing that, because Louis's execution meant the end of the French monarchy, Washington should suspend the 1778 treaty with France until it became clear what government France would have. Jefferson penned an opinion refuting Hamilton's arguments; he insisted that, because the treaty was with the French nation, not its monarchy, it was still valid. Impressed, Washington and the cabinet endorsed his view.

On the heels of the Neutrality Proclamation, Edmond Charles Edouard Genet, the new French minister to the United States, ignited a crisis of his own. Arrogant and reckless, insisting that the two republics were allied against monarchy and tyranny, "Citizen" Genet (using a Revolutionary French title intended to dramatize the idea of equality) traveled around the nation, raising money to fund French ships that would attack British merchant vessels and enlisting American sailors to serve on those ships. His efforts threatened to draw

Thomas Jefferson was grateful for King Louis XVI's decision to support the American cause in the Revolution, but he thought the king was foolish and incompetent. The French Revolution toppled Louis and his queen, Marie Antoinette, from their thrones, and the revolutionary government later executed them by the guillotine.

the United States into war. Hamilton and the Federalists argued that the President should demand Genet's recall.

Jefferson and the Republicans at first tried both to defend Genet and to rein him in. In the process, Jefferson—torn by conflicts among his loyalty to France, his patriotism, and his growing impatience with Genet's antics—was less than candid with Washington about what and when he knew of Genet's doings. Finally, Genet declared that he would "appeal from the President to the people"; that is, that he would go over Washington's head and make his case to the voters. The threat was an explosive one, and it put Jefferson and the Pennsylvania Republican politician Alexander James Dallas, the only eyewitnesses of Genet's vow, in a politically desperate position. At the same time that Jefferson glumly assured Madison that Genet had indeed vowed to go to the people, he insisted that the Frenchman was confused about American politics and government and had intended, rather, only to appeal to Congress. In Jefferson's eyes, however, Genet had come to be a dreadful liability to France and to the Republican cause in America. Finally, he joined the rest of the cabinet in backing the President's demand that the French recall Genet. At the same time, Madison carefully orchestrated a Republican campaign to distance themselves from Genet and to persuade the people that the Federalists were manipulating the crisis for partisan effect.

These controversies spurred Hamilton to write another series of newspaper essays, signed "Pacificus," defending the President's broad power to make foreign policy. Aghast, on July 7, 1793, Jefferson begged Madison, "For god's sake, my dear Sir, take up your pen, select the most striking heresies, and cut him to peices in the face of the public." At Jefferson's urging, Madison, writing as "Helvidius" (a pen name taken from the Roman senator Helvidius Priscus, who defended republican government in the days of the Emperor Vespasian and paid for his courage with his life), defended Congress's authority over foreign affairs.

For Jefferson, however, the Genet affair was the last straw. Once more, his letters praised private life and denounced the tortures of public service, just as they had after his bruising governorship of Virginia. On January 5, 1794, despite one last attempt by Washington to persuade him to stay in office, he left Philadelphia, swearing that he was finished with politics.

With Jefferson gone, Washington no longer could sustain his cabinet's balance between two strong advocates of competing viewpoints. Edmund Randolph, who sided with Jefferson, succeeded him as secretary of state; but, in 1795, Randolph resigned, amid charges (disputed to this day) that he was a tool of France's Revolutionary government. Thereafter, Washington increasingly relied on Hamilton and his supporters, and Jefferson, Madison, and their allies came to see Washington as the head—or, some charged, the figurehead—of a Federalist faction.

Ironically, Jefferson's resignation may have fueled the fires of partisan divisions of the late 1790s. Jefferson, however, was too busy congratulating himself on escaping public life to think about his decision's unintended consequences. Once more he was a gentleman planter, surrounded by his family and his books, exploring the world of ideas so dear to him.

TOUCHING EARTH
(1794–1797)

On January 5, 1794, Thomas Jefferson set out from Philadelphia for Virginia. Within two weeks, on January 18, he was back at Monticello. Soon he was penning letters to his friends rejoicing at his retirement and assuring them that he was finished with newspapers and politics. On February 13, 1794, he assured James Madison, "We are in a state of great quiet, having no public news to agitate us." He had grimmer news to report as well. He was shaken by the dilapidated condition of his house, Monticello, and by the decline of his plantations. On May 14, 1794, he fretted to Washington, "I find on a more minute examination of my lands than the short visits heretofore made to them permitted, that a ten years' abandonment of them to the ravages of overseers, has brought on them a degree of degradation far beyond what I expected."

At the same time that he blamed his overseers for having let things fall apart while he was gone, he implied that his entanglement with public business, the cause of his absence, was the true source of these problems. Thus, when his successor as secretary of state, Edmund Randolph, tried to lure him back into public life by proposing to name him as a special envoy to Spain to negotiate a new treaty, he politely but bluntly said no. On September 7, 1794, Jefferson wrote to Randolph, "No circumstance, my dear Sir, will ever more tempt me to engage in anything public. I thought myself perfectly fixed in this determination when I left Philadelphia, but every day and hour since has added to its inflexibility."

Opening his long-neglected farm and garden books, Jefferson decided first to develop a new plan for rotating his crops. He hoped to abandon tobacco, which brought a good return in the export market but left the soil empty of nutrients; instead, he would grow wheat and other crops that would improve his land and be sold at home. Riding around his plantations, he also became disgusted with the rail fences that he had used to mark off his fields. Not only were they ugly, but looking after them required too much work. Instead, he hit on the idea of planting rows of trees. In the next three years, he directed the planting of 1,157 peach trees, as well as cherry and apple trees, in dozens of varieties. His plan provided permanent, "natural" borders for his fields, heightened his plantations' beauty, and guaranteed a steady supply of his favorite fruits.

In a typical year, 1795, Monticello followed the cycle of plantation life under Jefferson's attentive gaze. In January and February, his slaves slaughtered livestock for the rest of the year, burned charcoal for the forges, mended fences, and cleared new farmland. That year, Jefferson also ordered them to prepare for a gargantuan new task—making enough bricks for the planned renovations of Monticello. In the spring, he focused on his extensive gardens. In March, his field hands began to plow the fields and spread them with manure, to plant red clover, and to bottle cider, a favorite drink, which they had laid up in large wooden casks the previous fall. In April and May, Jefferson kept an anxious eye on his apple and peach orchards, lest a late frost deprive him of a desirable harvest.

His slaves began planting corn, harvesting peas, and sowing buckwheat, which that fall they would plow under to improve the soil for the crop of regular winter wheat. By the end of May, they harvested cherries and strawberries. In the summer, they harvested barley and wheat, but in August, torrential rains ruined Jefferson's corn crop, and harsh sun threatened to ruin his tobacco harvest and scorch the hay in the fields. Jefferson looked forward to the chance to harvest his grapes and make wine, though he knew that Virginia wines would have to mature for decades before they could match the quality of French wines, which he admired greatly.

In the fall, his slaves harvested what they could salvage of the corn and wheat and began to make the next year's cider and peach brandy. That winter, they protected the fig trees against the coming snows, wrapping them securely in straw rope. Winter at Monticello was a time when Jefferson, his family, and his slaves could do nothing more than safeguard their health and wait out the cold.

As he struggled to bring order and system to his long-neglected farming, Jefferson ventured into new territory. He spent months devising and experimenting with a mechanical threshing machine, which would make it easier to separate the grain from the chaff of harvested wheat. He also designed a new type of plow that would cut through the soil more swiftly and with less resistance, making it easier and more efficient to cultivate land.

Finally, in a move that might have brought derisive laughter from Hamilton, who had reason to remember Jefferson's hostility to his "Report on Manufactures," Jefferson established a small nail-making factory at Monticello. He directed his overseers to assign to the task slave boys between 10 and 16 years of age, who were too young to work alongside the field hands. He took careful notes of their rate of production, rewarding those who turned out the most nails with the least waste of raw material. At first, he was turning a small profit, enough every three months to pay for that period's outlay on groceries. However, in early 1796, to his dismay, a flood of cheap British nails deluged Virginia,

Jefferson kept detailed records of his purchases of such luxury goods as fine wines, of which he was particularly fond. His ledgers also document his free-spending habits, which regularly outstripped his income.

absorbing much of the market for Jefferson's homemade product. In trying to sell his nails, he faced another, age-old American problem: his customers' lack of ready cash. For the next 20 years, Jefferson had to worry about pestering those who had bought his nails but not yet paid for them.

Family concerns also preoccupied Jefferson, who was now in his early fifties. A doting grandfather, he happily watched over Martha Jefferson Randolph's first son, Thomas Jefferson Randolph, a healthy, energetic toddler. Sadly, in

July 1795 Martha's infant daughter Eleanor died, and her husband, Thomas Mann Randolph, suffered bouts of depression and irrational anger, of the kind that beset other members of the Randolph family. Jefferson's younger daughter, Maria, was in low spirits and delicate health. Martha was tough enough to survive Jefferson's flood of well-meant advice, but it wore the more sensitive Maria down, making her increasingly timid and frail. Even after her marriage in 1798 to John Wayles Eppes (a distant cousin who had read law with Jefferson in Philadelphia in the early 1790s), she remained more fragile in body and mind than her sister. Unfortunately, Jefferson never could see the problems besetting Maria, let alone realize that his lectures made things worse for her.

Jefferson's retreat from the contentious, bruising world of politics and his happy immersion in the world of family, friends, and farming form part of a recurring pattern in his life. The refuge he found at home actually consisted of two small realms, one nesting within the other. The innermost realm was that of family. Within the intimate sphere defined by his family, Jefferson could experience the full measure of love and moral support that he craved. That this realm of family was peopled mostly by women had special significance, for Jefferson expected the women in his life to repay his love and devotion not only with love and devotion in return but also with deference. Jefferson never welcomed women's active participation in public life; the only woman with whom he managed even partial comfort in discussing politics was the formidable Abigail Adams.

Surrounding this safe haven was another, less intimate world than that of family, but in its own way just as restorative and reassuring—that of polite society. Jefferson assembled around himself a circle of trusted friends (such as Madison, Monroe, and Short) in whom he could confide and with whom he could share his range of interests, enthusiasms, and pursuits.

Thus, when in 1781 Jefferson turned his back on public life after his difficult and humiliating time as Virginia's governor, he had taken refuge behind these bulwarks of family and friends. The death of his wife, Martha, in 1782 shattered his innermost refuge, but grimly he set out to rebuild it while once more venturing into the world of politics and diplomacy. In 1794, once more spurning the world of public life, he embraced retirement, gathering around him his family and friends and resuming the role of a Virginia gentleman planter. In this time, he often expressed the hope that his friends might relocate to the vicinity of Monticello; this yearning expressed his desire to buttress his treasured refuges of family and friends. His repeated retreats to Monticello—in 1781, in 1794, and finally in 1809—make even more sense when we see them not just as flights from the remorseless struggles of politics but as flights to realms in which he felt safe, admired, respected, and, above all, loved.

Jefferson's retirement gave him the first chance in more than a decade to reconsider Monticello with critical eyes, measuring the house that he had built in the 1770s against his impressions of European architecture in the 1780s. Jefferson had a local reputation as a talented architect; his friends and neighbors often consulted him on building or rebuilding their houses. Recalling the country houses and Roman ruins that he had studied, he determined to transform Monticello into something that his idol, the 16th-century Italian architect Andrea Palladio, would have admired. Just as important, he wanted to have a house that one could live in year-round, unlike Palladio's country villas, which were for summer use only.

At his drawing board, he sketched a domed two-story building that, from the outside, would seem only one story tall. The new Monticello also would be twice its former width, more than doubling the size of his library and adding guest rooms. Meanwhile, his slaves were busily making bricks, and Jefferson prepared to have them pull down much of the original house. These were the first steps of a massive building program that continued, on and off (when his finances permitted), for nearly 30 years, and became his chief hobby—and one of his chief financial burdens.

Jefferson did the designing, but his slaves did the work, ranging from the making of bricks and the pulling down or putting up of walls to skilled carpentry and furniture making. Although Jefferson lived on a daily basis with the reality of slavery, he shaped his life to have as few face-to-face confrontations with slavery as possible.

As with so much of his life and thought, he arranged a system of neat compartments to keep separate things that he believed ought to remain separate. Some of Monticello's most distinctive features shielded the plantation's slave life from Jefferson's gaze, in ways similar to those followed by

Jefferson used dumb-waiters such as this one at Monticello to set a tone of friendly, informal conversation at meals by ensuring that slaves did not interrupt him and his guests.

other planters, but always bearing the stamp of his own architectural ingenuity. For example, the dumbwaiters—tiered serving shelves mounted on small casters so that they could be rolled about—enabled house servants to bring food to the dining room without intruding on conversation there. A slave would wheel a dumbwaiter to the dining room, latch it to the rotating dining-room door, and then turn so that the door would carry the laden dumbwaiter to Jefferson and his guests, who would serve themselves.

On either side of the fireplace was a wine dumbwaiter, connecting the dining room to the wine cellar directly below; a slave would load the required wine bottle into a box and hoist it by a pulley up to the dining room. Jefferson would open the door of the wine dumbwaiter, remove the bottle, and offer it to his guests. Further, the estate's landscaping and covered walkways blocked the main house's direct view of the slave quarters.

In another practice designed to shield himself from the realities of slavery at Monticello, Jefferson increasingly left supervision of farming to his overseers. He remained at the main house, surrounded and served by the house slaves, most of them members or relatives of the Hemings family, who were less obviously black than were the field hands. The Hemingses had white and black ancestors; indeed, Sally Hemings's ancestors were mostly white. She was responsible for tending Jefferson's bedchamber and clothing, and gradually was given extensive authority over running the main house.

In 1795, Jefferson recorded in his farm book the first child born to Sally Hemings, who then was 22 years old. This daughter, Harriet, died two years later, in 1797. During the next 14 years, Jefferson recorded the births of five more children to Sally Hemings, all but one of whom grew to adulthood. William Beverly Hemings was born in 1798; another daughter (unnamed) was born in 1799 and died later that year; a second Harriet was born in 1801; James Madison Hemings was born in 1805; and Thomas Eston

Hemings was born in 1809. All of Sally Hemings's sons were known by their middle names: Beverly, Madison, and Eston.

Was Thomas Jefferson the father of Sally Hemings's children? Though we lack definite proof, circumstantial evidence frames a plausible answer. Jefferson's farm books show that every time Sally Hemings gave birth, he had been in the vicinity nine months before. Also, memories and oral traditions preserved for generations among the Hemings family point to their descent from Jefferson and Hemings, and these memories and oral traditions fit with information recorded in Jefferson's private papers. Further, all of Sally Hemings's children received names with close links to the Jefferson family, something not true of the other slaves born at Monticello. Jefferson never publicly avowed any relationship with Hemings, nor did he acknowledge her children as his. When rumors of a relationship between them broke in the press during his first term as President, however, he never explicitly denied them.

When Jefferson left Philadelphia in January 1794, he swore that he was finished with politics, and he tried hard to keep his word. Like the mythical wrestler Antaeus, Jefferson seemed to revive himself and restore his energy by touching earth. Even so, his continuing anxiety for the future of the United States and the fate of the Revolution—and his tendency to develop an increasing interest in the place where he was not and the things that he was not doing—again reasserted themselves.

His friends continued to keep him informed of the latest political developments, hoping to woo him back into public life. In the fall of 1794, the news that Washington and Hamilton had led a force of 15,000 soldiers through the Pennsylvania countryside to quell the Whiskey Rebellion appalled Jefferson. In his view, Hamilton was using a standing army to enforce federal law (a tax on whiskey) against a group of angry farmers, which was a dictatorial policy that endangered the principle of civilian supremacy over the military. In August 1795, he learned of the treaty that Chief Justice John Jay had negotiated with Great Britain—a treaty that, to his dismay, seemed far too generous to the former mother country. Jefferson therefore denounced it in his private letters, and he cheered the vain efforts of Madison and his allies in the House to block the treaty from going into effect. And yet, even as he did so, he continued to insist that he was nothing more than a private citizen.

By the end of 1795, however, Jefferson was beginning to consider returning to public life; he again subscribed to newspapers and increasingly expressed his views on current issues. On December 31, 1795, he wrote to his old ally William Branch Giles,

> [W]here the principle of difference is as substantial and strongly pronounced as between the republicans & the Monocrats [monarchists] of our country, I hold it as honorable to take a firm & decided part, and as immoral to pursue a middle line, as between the parties of Honest men, & Rogues, into which every country is divided.

Jefferson argued that Americans faced something beyond a mere party division. It was, rather, a stark contrast between supporters and opponents of the American Revolution's core principles. Jefferson was convinced that his opponents were backers of kingly government, and that he and his friends were champions of republican liberty. By monarchists or "monocrats," he meant supporters of a strong general government and of debt-based public finance, like those found in Great Britain. Such measures, he feared, would undermine republican virtue and bring real monarchy and aristocracy to America—a vast scheme of oppression that it was his duty, and the duty of all honest men, to resist.

Even now, however, Jefferson insisted on remaining in retirement. It required gentle pressure from Madison and other political allies to revive his willingness to take an active part in the nation's public life. The key event was the impending 1796 Presidential election.

Unlike modern Presidential contests, which begin years before the actual election, the 1796 campaign did not even start until September of that year, when Washington announced his decision to retire from the Presidency at the end of his second term. Washington never delivered his famed "Farewell Address" as a speech. Instead, he published it as an open letter in the *Pennsylvania Packet,* on September 19, 1796. A day later, on September 20, the Philadelphia *Aurora,* the fiery anti-administration newspaper, declared:

> It requires no talent at divination to decide who will be candidates for the chair. THOMAS JEFFERSON & JOHN ADAMS will be the men, & whether we shall have at the head of our executive a steadfast friend to the Rights of the People, or an advocate for hereditary power and distinctions, the people of the United States are soon to decide.

Jefferson's backers agreed with the *Aurora* that the Virginian was their choice for the Presidency. Madison already had hinted to Jefferson that Republicans were prepared to unite behind him, only to learn that Jefferson wanted Madison to be the standard-bearer. Once he had talked Jefferson out of that idea, Madison and other Republican leaders sought a way to involve Jefferson in the campaign without risking his flat refusal. On September 29, 1796, for example, Madison advised Monroe, "I have not seen Jefferson and have thought it best to present him no opportunity of protesting to his friends against being embarked in the contest." The mechanism they used was an informal gathering of leading Republicans in the House and Senate, known as a caucus, which agreed to back Jefferson and Senator Aaron Burr of New York. Thus, without direct effort on his part, Jefferson became the Republicans' preferred candidate in the first contested Presidential election in American history.

The election of 1796, like the two that preceded it, took place under rules very different from today's. Taking account of rivalries among the states and regions, the electoral college required each state's Presidential electors to vote for two candidates, at least one of whom had to be from a different state. The Constitution's framers and ratifiers believed that, because of rivalry among the states, most elections would generate three or even four candidates, from whom the House of Representatives would pick the President; they expected the House to decide four out of five elections.

The first two elections, in 1789 and 1792, turned out differently, however; Washington's popularity led to his unanimous election and reelection. Also, the electoral college did not take account of the rise of partisan divisions spanning state borders, such as those separating Federalists from Republicans. Even so, these partisan alliances were not hard and fast. Northerners preferred to vote for Northerners and Southerners preferred to vote for Southerners, even if that meant voting for a Federalist and a Republican from their own region. Thus, competing partisan and sectional influences played a game of tug-of-war in 1796.

Elections were contests about character and reputation as much as policy and party. Thus, Jefferson's foes attacked his public and private records. For example, "A Southern Planter" published a broadside—a printed wall poster— denouncing Jefferson because of his opposition to slavery and his supposed support for abolition. The broadside reprinted antislavery quotations from *Notes on the State of Virginia* and from Jefferson's 1791 letter to Benjamin Banneker, and noted the plan of St. George Tucker, a leading Virginia lawyer known to favor Jefferson, by which the United States would buy and free all the slaves. The broadside concluded, "If this wild project succeeds, under the auspices of Thomas Jefferson, President of the United States, and three hundred thousand slaves are set free in Virginia, farewel[l] to the safety, prosperity, the importance, perhaps the very existence of the Southern States."

Other critics charged that Jefferson was an atheist enemy to all religion; that he had been a cowardly and inept governor

Isaac Jefferson was born at Monticello and spent much of his life as a slave of Thomas Jefferson. A skilled blacksmith whom Jefferson named first manager of Monticello's nailery, Isaac Jefferson later gave a series of interviews recording his memories of Jefferson's life, appearance, and habits as the master of Monticello.

of Virginia; that his resignation from Washington's cabinet had damaged the nation in a time of foreign peril; and that he was unsuited to the demands of the Presidency. In a series of newspaper essays later collected as a pamphlet, South Carolina Federalist William Loughton Smith ridiculed Jefferson's claims to philosophical and scientific learning; even if Jefferson deserved those merits, Smith concluded, "of all beings, a philosopher makes the worst politician" because a philosopher lacked the seriousness and determination to wield power effectively. Another South Carolina Federalist, Robert Goodloe Harper, denounced Jefferson as "a weak, wavering, indecisive character" not fit to be "the first magistrate of a great nation."

Yet another favorite Federalist charge was that Jefferson was an uncritical admirer of France who would be too dazzled by the French to defend American interests. Unfortunately, the injudicious French minister to the United States, Pierre Adet, provided support for these charges by implying that his government preferred Jefferson to Adams. Ironically, Adet's scheming confirmed Jefferson's earlier worry that France and Britain would try to interfere in American Presidential elections. Another irony was that, on December 31, 1796, Adet warned his government that he doubted how true a friend of France Jefferson would be:

> Mr. Jefferson likes us because he detests England; he seeks to draw near us because he fears us less than Great Britain; but he might change his opinion of us tomorrow, if tomorrow Great Britain should cease to inspire his fears. Jefferson, although a friend of liberty and learning, although an admirer of the efforts we have made to break our bonds and dispel the cloud of ignorance which weighs down the human race, Jefferson, I say, is American, and, as such, he cannot be sincerely our friend. An American is the born enemy of all the European peoples.

In this era, Presidential elections were decided by the elections of state legislatures, which in turn chose Presidential electors. There was no one day on which the people turned out to vote for President and Vice President, but all the states' Presidential electors cast their votes nationwide on the same day. By the end of 1796, the results of the electoral vote were public knowledge. Adams won with a narrow majority of 71 electoral votes; Jefferson was second with 68, only three votes behind Adams, thus becoming Vice President. Thomas Pinckney of South Carolina, Adams's fellow Federalist, was a respectable third, with 59, and Aaron Burr finished a distant fourth, with 30. Burr felt betrayed and humiliated by the Virginians who had talked him into standing for election with Jefferson; as far as he could tell, southern Republicans had not kept their promises to back him.

Jefferson did not mention the election in his correspondence. At the end of November, in a letter thanking his son-in-law Thomas Mann Randolph for news of Virginia's electoral results, he declared his hope that he might be elected to the Vice Presidency rather than the Presidency. First, he sincerely wished to take second place to his old friend John Adams. Second, the Vice Presidency would give him more time at home with his family and his books. Third, as he told Madison on December 17, 1796, "Let those come to the helm who think they can steer clear of the difficulties. I have no confidence in myself for the undertaking."

Jefferson drafted a friendly congratulatory letter to Adams, but he asked Madison for his comments, and Madison advised him not to send it. Madison noted that some of Jefferson's phrasing might offend Adams, who was notably thin-skinned, and that Jefferson's heavy-handed, joking references to Hamilton's scheming were unnecessary and inappropriate. Finally, Madison worried that Jefferson's gushing expressions of friendship and support for Adams risked tying Jefferson to Adams's policies and alienating Jefferson's Republican supporters. Jefferson agreed with Madison's judgment and kept his draft among his papers while he prepared to return to the city from which he had departed with such pleasure three years before.

CHAPTER

7

"THE REIGN OF WITCHES" (1797–1801)

In March 1797, Thomas Jefferson hoped to skip his own swearing-in as Vice President out of his dislike of any ceremony that seemed monarchical, but his friends persuaded him at the last minute that he could not do so without drawing criticism. His hopes to enter Philadelphia quietly, as a private citizen, were dashed when Republican supporters met him with brass bands and cheering rallies.

Vice President Jefferson's principal official duty was to preside over the Senate's deliberations. Like Adams, he took this duty seriously, but his way was more effective than Adams's approach had been. Adams had been an activist president of the Senate, throwing himself into debate and trying to steer the Senate's conduct of its business. Frustrated when his efforts failed, as they often did, he complained to Abigail Adams that the Vice Presidency was "the most insignificant office ever the invention of man contrived or his imagination conceived." By contrast, Jefferson let senators conduct their own debates, limiting himself to deciding issues of procedure; as a result, he found his new post "honorable and easy."

Given his extensive knowledge of parliamentary law and procedure, which he had studied for nearly four decades,

Jefferson was superbly qualified to serve as president of the Senate. At the beginning of his term, he wrote to George Wythe for guidance, claiming that he was out of practice, but Wythe confessed that he was rusty on those subjects as well. For these reasons, while presiding over the Senate, Jefferson compiled a small book based on the "Parliamentary Pocket-Book" that he had prepared for his own use. In 1800, he revised and published this book, giving it the modest title *A Manual of Parliamentary Practice.* In this volume, he organized for the Senate's use the rules and precedents of parliamentary procedure, accompanied by extensive citations to and discussions of British authorities. Its pages synthesized years of research in a form that blended clarity of explanation with literary grace.

Neither Jefferson nor his biographers claimed it as a full-length book or a work of major importance, but Federalists and Republicans alike hailed his *Manual* as a valuable guide on how to conduct business in a legislative assembly. It went through many editions and has remained in print to this day. In fact, the U.S. House of Representatives still uses it as an authority for deciding issues of procedure. It stands beside *Robert's Rules of Order* as the most useful guide to parliamentary procedure ever written.

While presiding over the Senate, Jefferson took the opportunity to observe its members. In the process, he amassed a thorough knowledge of many of the new nation's politicians, which he drew on in later years, and further developed his mastery of collegial politics.

Because the Vice Presidency was not a demanding office, Jefferson often could devote his energies to more congenial pursuits. In 1797, he was named the third president of the American Philosophical Society, the leading organization for the promotion of science in the United States, founded by Benjamin Franklin. Accepting this office (succeeding Franklin and the astronomer David Rittenhouse, both cherished friends), Jefferson disclaimed

First used as the home of Congress in 1800, the unfinished Capitol stood in lonely splendor amid the mud, swamps, and hills of Washington, D.C., the new nation's permanent capital.

his qualifications for the post: "I feel no qualification for this distinguished post, but a sincere zeal for all the objects of our institution, and an ardent desire to see knowledge so disseminated through the mass of mankind, that it may, at length, reach even the extremes of society, beggars and kings." Even so, he became an active, eager leader of the Philosophical Society, promoting the full range of American scientific research.

Jefferson also took pride in sharing with the society his own discoveries, including his description of fossils discovered on land that he owned and which he was the first scientist to examine. Unfortunately, in one such case he was misled by the tall tales recounted to him by John and Archibald Stuart, who brought the fossils to him. They told him that they had seen carvings on nearby rocks of a large lion, presumably the same animal that left the bones they were now sending him. Further, they declared, hunters had heard the roaring of a great lionlike creature in the wilderness—suggesting that these were the bones of a creature still living in the wilds of Virginia. Jefferson identified the bones he had received as foot and leg bones, and a few claws from the paw. Hence, he gave the creature the name Megalonyx, or "great claw," and assured the Philosophical Society that it was a great carnivore like a lion.

After Jefferson submitted his paper, but before he presented it at a meeting of the society, he discovered that a French scientist, Georges Cuvier, had examined a similar skeleton found in Paraguay, and had identified the creature as some sort of great sloth, not a carnivore. Jefferson realized that Cuvier's sloth was almost identical to his Megalonyx. He swiftly edited his paper to take account of Cuvier's findings, stepping back from some of his own claims. In 1798, he announced another major find to the society—bones of a mammoth, also discovered in Virginia. He also presented papers discussing such technological innovations as a hand-operated threshing machine and his own improvements on the plow.

In a more painful controversy, politics intruded on Jefferson's devotion to natural history. A political foe forced him to revisit one of the most moving passages of *Notes on the State of Virginia,* in which he set forth his admiration for the eloquence of Native Americans, such as Chief Logan. In 1774, Logan had waged a bitter war against colonial Virginia because, he claimed, his entire family was murdered by Captain Michael Cresap; at the war's close, he gave a speech that Jefferson described as a classic worthy of the Greek orator Demosthenes or the Roman senator and consul Marcus Tullius Cicero.

Unfortunately for Jefferson, Cresap's son-in-law was Luther Martin of Maryland, a leading Federalist politician; Martin was determined to defend his father-in-law's reputation and to strike a blow against his party's leading foe. For years, he and Jefferson disputed whether Jefferson's account of the murder of Logan's family was true. Martin charged, among other things, that Jefferson had suppressed a letter sent to him by General George Rogers Clark bearing out Cresap's version of events. To this day, historians argue about whether Jefferson or Martin was right about what happened to Logan's family at Cresap's hands, though most historians favor Logan's (and Jefferson's) account. Federalists backed Martin, however, adding this charge to the attacks they made on Jefferson based on his scientific interests and research.

Politics disturbed Jefferson's serenity in other ways, making his time as Vice President notably unhappy. Because the election of 1796 had confirmed him as leader of the Republican opposition, and the most likely challenger to President John Adams in 1800, Federalist politicians and pamphleteers kept up a constant fire of vicious abuse, their favorite charge being that he was hostile to religion and morality.

In May 1797, in newspapers arriving from London, Federalists found a weapon against Jefferson of amazing effectiveness—one from his own pen, though garbled by a series of translations.

On April 24, 1796, as he was preparing to reenter public life, Jefferson wrote to his old friend Philip Mazzei, an Italian whom he had brought to Monticello long before to help him develop American grapes and wines. Jefferson gave Mazzei a heated sketch of the American political scene. He denounced the "Anglican monarchical, & aristocratical party... whose avowed object is to draw over us the substance, as they have already done the forms, of the British government." Though he was sure that the people opposed these steps, Jefferson fretted: "Against us are the Executive, the Judiciary, ... all the officers of the government, all who want to be officers, all timid men who prefer the calm of despotism to the boisterous sea of liberty...." He then wrote a sentence that haunted him for the rest of his life: "It would give you a fever were I to name to you the apostates who have gone over to these heresies, men who were Samsons in the field & Solomons in the council, but who have had their heads shorn by the harlot England."

The well-meaning but indiscreet Mazzei translated Jefferson's letter into Italian and published it in a local newspaper. A French newspaper translated the Italian version into French. This French translation found its way to Britain, where newspapers retranslated the French translation of the Italian translation back into English. This corrupted translation of a translation of a translation made its way back across the Atlantic and exploded in American newspapers. Federalists read it aloud in Congress and berated Jefferson in the press. Their main charge was that he had stabbed the revered George Washington in the back. Washington, they claimed, was the target of Jefferson's taunting phrases about "Samsons in the field" and "Solomons in the council." Jefferson, they insisted, had turned on the one man whom all Americans could trust and revere.

Jefferson was tormented by the republications of his letter and by Federalist demands that he avow or deny it. He felt that the published version garbled his meaning, but that, for his views to be understood, he would have to publish a large mass of confidential information from his private papers, which would make his situation even worse. He did differ with Washington, but he believed that to explain all the points on which they agreed and disagreed would serve no purpose. Thus, no matter how loudly his critics demanded that he explain his letter to Mazzei, he maintained a dignified, wounded silence.

The Mazzei controversy was a sideshow to the larger issues of public policy and foreign affairs that preoccupied him and his countrymen in the first years of the Adams administration. For years, the constant state of war in Europe between Revolutionary France and its foes had divided American politicians and the American people. In the midst of these controversies, President Adams had made a series of speeches bitterly denouncing France. In late 1797 and early 1798, however, it seemed that the United States might be able to restore friendly relations with France while preserving peace with Great Britain. France's radical government had toppled, replaced by a more conservative regime known as the

"THE ASPECT OF OUR POLITICS HAS WONDERFULLY CHANGED"

Writing to his friend Philip Mazzei on April 24, 1796, Jefferson exploded in frustration and anger at the politics of the 1790s. Mazzei published the letter without Jefferson's permission in an Italian translation; others translated his translation into French, and the French version into English. The English version turned up in American newspapers, embarrassing Jefferson.

The aspect of our politics has wonderfully changed since you left us. In place of that noble love of liberty, & republican government which carried us triumphantly thro' the war, an Anglican monarchical, & aristocratical party has sprung up, whose avowed object is to draw over us the substance, as they have already done the forms, of the British government. The main body of our citizens, however, remain true to their republican principles; the whole landed interest is republican, and so is a great mass of talents. Against us are the Executive, the Judiciary, two out of three branches of the legislature, all the officers of the government, all who want to be officers, all timid men who prefer the calm of despotism to the boisterous sea of liberty, British merchants & Americans trading on British capitals, speculators & holders in the banks & public funds, a contrivance invented for the purposes of corruption, & for assimilating us in all things to the rotten as well as the sound parts of the British model. It would give you a fever were I to name to you the apostates who have gone over to these heresies, men who were Samsons in the field & Solomons in the council, but who have had their heads shorn by the harlot England. In short, we are likely to preserve the liberty we have obtained only by unremitting labors & perils. But we shall preserve them; and our mass of weight & wealth on the good side is so great, as to leave no danger that force will ever be attempted against us. We have only to awake and snap the Lilliputian cords with which they have been entangling us during the first sleep which succeeded our labors.

Directory. For a time, this change had stilled the wars raging in Europe. Taking advantage of this chance to settle the outstanding American disputes with France, Adams named a delegation to negotiate with the French foreign minister, Charles-Maurice de Talleyrand-Périgord (known as Talleyrand). The President chose two Federalists, Charles Cotesworth Pinckney of South Carolina and John Marshall of Virginia, and one Republican, Elbridge Gerry of Massachusetts.

When Pinckney, Marshall, and Gerry arrived in France, they met repeated delays and excuses, until three midlevel French officials (whom the Americans cloaked in their report as X, Y, and Z) approached them. These men demanded that the United States apologize for President Adams's angry words from 1797, and they suggested that the Americans could make the wheels of French government turn more swiftly and favorably with a few good-sized sums of money put into the right hands. It was never clear whether those hands were their own, or Talleyrand's, or all of them.

The Americans reacted with anger; Pinckney said, "No! no! not a sixpence!"—a phrase that politicians transformed into the electrifying slogan "Millions for defense, but not one cent for tribute!" The commissioners drew up a report for President Adams, and Marshall traveled home with it. On his arrival in Philadelphia, Federalists stage-managed a gala welcome for Marshall. Then, springing a trap on the Republicans, President Adams released the envoys' full report, disclosing the French attempt to extort a bribe from the United States. The news spread swiftly, outraging the American people.

The XYZ Affair caught Jefferson, Madison, and their Republican allies—still warm friends to France and suspicious adversaries of Britain—by surprise. Taken aback by the French officials' greed, they could not deny that the French had insulted American honor, though the Directory regarded the Americans' anger as naive and silly. But Jefferson and his supporters feared how the Federalists might use the

In this cartoon, the American eagle exposes Thomas Jefferson as a foe of American constitutional government and an admirer of the turbulence and terror of Revolutionary France. Jefferson is dropping his 1796 letter to Philip Mazzei, which found its way into American newspapers and gave Federalists ammunition to charge that Jefferson had unfairly denounced the revered George Washington.

THE PROVIDENTIAL DETECTION

controversy. They suspected that Adams, stampeded by senators and representatives allied with Hamilton, might use the dispute as a pretext to launch a war with France. Events soon confirmed their fears.

While American and French warships clashed on the high seas, President Adams called for, and Congress enacted, a sweeping series of measures preparing for war between the two countries. First, the Federalists set out to enlarge the American army and navy, and created a Navy Department having cabinet rank. Second, they took other steps designed to protect what we would call national security. These steps included the Alien and Sedition Acts, which, Republicans charged, the Federalists copied from British measures enacted in 1795.

The Federalists backing these laws feared the flood of refugees from Ireland and France pouring into American cities. These men and women supposedly brought with them dangerous, revolutionary ideas that threatened to undermine religion and order in America. Responding to that alleged threat, the Alien Act extended from 7 to 14 years the time that foreigners ("aliens") had to live in the United States before they could become citizens; it and the Alien Enemies Act also gave the government sweeping powers to deport anyone not a citizen of the United States. Republicans had welcomed these refugees, many of whom had become pamphleteers and editors of Republican newspapers. Thus, Republicans saw the threat that aliens could be deported as a dangerous blow to American liberty.

The Sedition Act also seemed to endanger liberty. It targeted anyone who criticized the government or specific officials of the government. In Britain, the common law recognized a crime called seditious libel, speaking or publishing criticism of the government or its officials. It did not matter whether the criticism was true or not; in fact, the legal maxim was, "the greater the truth, the greater the libel."

The American Sedition Act of 1798 differed from British law in two key respects. It did not allow the government to prevent someone from publishing something ("prior restraint"), and it allowed the defendant to argue that the publication was true and published for good motives. Federalist advocates of the act argued that it was vital to protect the honor and reputation of the government and of those who held office under it. They insisted that the Constitution and the government it authorized were so fragile that their future depended on the individuals who made up the government. To allow anyone to destroy their reputations, or the reputation of the government, was to risk bringing down the whole constitutional system.

Republicans disagreed. They insisted that the government was strong enough to survive public criticism, and that any government worthy of the name needed no laws banning dissent to prop it up. In their view, the Sedition Act threatened to strangle healthy, justified criticism of the government, the President, and other key officials—though specifically not Jefferson, for the statute left the Vice President off the list of officials who could not be criticized. Republicans pointed out this omission as one clue to the statute's political purpose. Another clue was that the statute would expire on March 3, 1801, which was the last day of the 6th Congress and of Adams's Presidency. The implication was clear. If the Federalists were to win a majority in the 7th Congress, to be elected in 1800, they could reenact the Sedition Act, but if they were swept from power, Republicans would not have the old federal statute to use against them.

Jefferson remained publicly silent, confining his criticism of the Alien and Sedition Acts to private letters and behind-the-scenes politicking. On July 4, 1798, just after the enactment of the Sedition Act, he wrote to the Virginia pamphleteer and planter John Taylor of Carolina:

> A little patience, and we shall see the reign of witches pass over, their spells dissolve, and the people, recovering their true sight, restore their government to it's true principles. It is true that in the mean time we are suffering deeply in spirit, and incurring the horrors of a war & long oppressions of enormous public debt. . . . If the game runs sometimes against us at home we must have patience till luck turns, & then we shall have an opportunity of winning back the principles we have lost, for this is a game where principles are the stake.

Jefferson also warned Taylor of the dangers of leaking his letters, lest they fall into the hands of Federalist mudslingers such as "Peter Porcupine" (the pen name of the English political writer and Federalist William Cobbett): "It is hardly necessary to caution you to let nothing of mine get before the public. A single sentence, got hold of by the Porcupines, will suffice to abuse & persecute me in their papers for months."

Jefferson opposed the Sedition Act because, in his view, the First Amendment took away the federal government's power to pass such a law. His ally, James Madison, agreed, but Madison went further, believing that no American government, federal or state, could enact such a law. Jefferson still believed that states could use their power to punish individuals for seditious libel under the old common law, and later, as President, he would act on these beliefs.

Angered by what they saw as a Federalist bid to establish tyranny, Jefferson and Madison tried to spur the states to resist the Alien and Sedition Acts. Jefferson drafted two sets of resolutions that Kentucky's legislature adopted in 1798 and 1799. His Kentucky Resolutions declared that a state could strike down, or nullify, unconstitutional federal laws, preventing them from having effect within its own borders. Jefferson's arguments carried him dangerously close to embracing secession—the idea that a state could leave the Union. Meanwhile, Madison penned resolutions that the Virginia legislature adopted in 1798. Stopping short of nullification, the Virginia Resolutions argued that a state could thrust itself between its own citizens and federal authority and ask the other states to consider whether the federal government was overstepping its legitimate powers—a doctrine known as interposition.

Jefferson and Madison hoped that the Kentucky and Virginia Resolutions would rally the states against the Federalists' unconstitutional actions, but every other state, North and South, rejected Virginia's and Kentucky's views. In 1800, Madison drafted the Virginia legislature's report reasserting Virginia's position that the Alien and Sedition Acts were unconstitutional, but he and Jefferson were disappointed that Virginia and Kentucky stood alone.

Jefferson agreed with other Republicans that the Federalists' conduct under the Alien and Sedition Acts should become a key issue of the 1800 campaign. To this end, he launched one of the most disreputable episodes of his career, one that, years later, cost him untold vexation and embarrassment. James Thomson Callender, a scandal-mongering journalist, had fled his native Scotland to avoid prosecution for seditious libel. In America, he joined the Republicans' ranks and poured forth essays and pamphlets thrashing the Federalists with venomous glee. Jefferson offered Callender private funding, belying his oft-repeated claim that he had nothing to do with what was appearing in the newspapers.

Overwhelmed by Jefferson's friendliness and support, Callender was spurred to greater efforts. As he expected, outraged Federalists prosecuted him for his writings against Adams. He stood trial in the U.S. Circuit Court for the District of Virginia. Under the first laws governing the federal courts, a Supreme Court Justice presided over each U.S. circuit court, in a practice known as "riding circuit." Presiding over Callender's trial was Associate Justice Samuel Chase of Maryland, a loyal Federalist. The irascible Chase found Callender's writings so infuriating that he did not even pretend to be impartial in conducting the trial. Swiftly convicted, fined, sentenced, jailed, and scolded by Chase from the bench, Callender became a prize exhibit in the Republican case that the Federalists were bent on establishing tyranny in America.

Gearing up for the 1800 election, the Virginians again formed a political alliance with New York Republican leaders Governor George Clinton and Aaron Burr, though Burr and Clinton were less enthusiastic about the alliance than they had been four years earlier. Now fully aware of the dangers of sectional division within their ranks, Republicans sought to bind one another to the cause by exchanging pledges of honor and mutual support, requiring them to vote lockstep for both of their candidates. By and large, that is what happened.

These preparations left the Jeffersonian Republicans ready to wage an effective campaign in 1800. Further, they got an unintended gift from their foes—a rupture in Federalist ranks that led to the virtual self-destruction of the Federalist partisan alliance.

The first falling domino was Adams's decision, announced on February 18, 1799, to name William Vans Murray, American minister to the Netherlands, to open peace talks with France. Later, Adams added two more diplomats to the mission: Chief Justice Oliver Ellsworth and Governor William R. Davie of North Carolina (after Patrick Henry declined to serve on grounds of poor health). Stirrings of resentment among Hamiltonian Federalists greeted Adams's decision; distrusting the French, they scorned Adams's peace policy as naive and dangerous. Jefferson and his allies felt that Adams's initiative was too little, too late.

The second domino was George Washington's death on December 15, 1799. While Washington was alive, the factions within the Federalist alliance kept an uneasy peace; his death brought their divisions into the open. Hamiltonian Federalists insisted on a warlike posture against France. Adams Federalists wanted to explore the prospects of peace with France. Adams bears much blame for this conflict, for he had done little to cement unity within Federalist ranks. He was often an absentee President, spending weeks at a time at his Massachusetts farm caring for his ailing wife. Also, he had kept Washington's cabinet members in office, despite their loyalty to Hamilton, because he worried that if he replaced them, others would think he was questioning Washington's judgment. While Adams was at home, his cabinet often asked Hamilton for advice and took direction from him, even meeting with him behind Adams's back.

In May of 1800, when Adams discovered this state of affairs, he exploded in wrath. First, he confronted Secretary of War James McHenry and forced him to resign; days later, he fired Secretary of State Timothy Pickering. The result was that the fragile bond holding Federalists together in the face of Republican opposition snapped. After a heated face-to-face confrontation with the President, Hamilton penned a furious pamphlet, "A Letter from Alexander Hamilton, Concerning the Public Conduct and Character of John

Adams, Esq., President of the United States," urging Federalists to abandon Adams for his running mate, Charles Cotesworth Pinckney of South Carolina, a hero of the XYZ Affair.

Hamilton had intended this pamphlet, which he published late that October, to circulate only among leading Federalists, but its contents found their way into the newspapers—allegedly through the machinations of Aaron Burr. Hamilton then republished his pamphlet, feeling that the damage had been done and some good might come of it; but the widespread publication of Hamilton's pamphlet damaged his and Adams's reputations and revealed the split in Federalist ranks to the nation.

As the Federalists disintegrated, the Republicans fought to hold themselves together in the face of rumors, such as the false report of Jefferson's sudden death, apparently a ploy to discourage his supporters from going to the polls. Because each state's legislature chose its Presidential electors, elections of state legislatures indicated how each state would vote in the Presidential contest. Given that each state followed a different electoral schedule, returns from the states dribbled into the national press through the summer and fall of 1800. In key states, Federalists and Republicans each sought to erode the other side's likely victories, suggesting that state legislatures divide their state's electoral votes in proportion to the Federalist and Republican strength in that state, or, by contrast, lump their votes in a "winner-take-all" system in states where their political strength was dominant.

The result of all the tugging and hauling was that the Republicans captured the Presidency and both houses of Congress. However, when in December 1800 the states' electoral votes were announced, the nation discovered that the Republicans' insistence that their electors vote for both candidates—a tactic intended to guard against sectional rivalry deciding the election—had worked too well.

Aaron Burr was admired and distrusted by nearly everyone who knew him. A leading New York politician, Burr helped Jefferson win the election of 1800, but lost Jefferson's trust and eventually was tried for treason.

Jefferson and Burr received 73 electoral votes each, with Adams and Pinckney finishing third and fourth.

In 1787–88, when the Constitution was adopted, most Americans expected most Presidential elections to give no candidate a majority. The electoral college would thin the field, not decide the election. Instead, the House of Representatives, with each state delegation having one vote, would choose the President and the Vice President. However, George Washington's two unanimous victories in 1789 and 1792, and John Adams's narrow victory in 1796, had seemed to show that the electoral college would decide Presidential elections. The test of experience shifted Americans' understandings away from their original expectations of how the

Constitution would work. Thus, in 1800 they were alarmed by a deadlock that, in 1788, they would have expected as a normal result.

The task of breaking the deadlock fell to the lame-duck House, which had a Federalist majority; the new, Republican House of Representatives would not convene until December 1801. This oddity should not have mattered, for the top two candidates were both Republicans, and Republicans expected Burr to declare that he would not even consider supplanting Jefferson as the people's choice. Indeed, Burr announced that he would defer to Jefferson, but he was irked by the Virginians' insistence that he refuse even to think about the Presidency for himself. He remembered how he had finished a distant fourth in 1796, and he still blamed Jefferson and Jefferson's friends for his poor showing. Besides, under the Constitution, Burr was in theory a candidate for the Presidency, and he thought that he was as qualified for that office as Jefferson was. Why should he accept the Virginians' demand that he declare himself, by implication, inferior to Jefferson and thus unworthy of the Presidency? This Burr refused to do.

Burr thought that he was behaving with due regard to his own character and reputation, but Jefferson's supporters were infuriated that Burr seemed to be challenging their hero. Driven frantic by fears that Burr would betray Jefferson, they began to suspect the worst—that Burr was intriguing with the defeated Federalists to capture the Presidency for himself and betray his party and its chief. Worse yet, rumors reached them that Federalists were pondering just that prospect.

On February 11, 1801, the House convened and heard the official report of the electoral deadlock. Then they cast ballots, state by state. Each vote ended with Jefferson just short of the majority of state delegations that the Constitution required. As the House struggled to resolve the deadlock, the demoralized Federalists debated what to do. They had no hope of electing Adams or Pinckney; some who loathed

Jefferson wondered if Burr would be willing to deal with them for the Presidency, so that they could preserve their role in national politics.

Meanwhile, in New York, Hamilton was shaken by the backfire of his pamphlet against Adams and aghast at the election's results. On December 13, 1800, President Adams wrote with bitter humor to his friend William Tudor, "Mr. Hamilton has carried his eggs to a fine market. The very two men of all the world that he was most jealous of are now placed over him." When Hamilton learned that Federalists were pondering a deal with Burr to prevent Jefferson's election, he fired off letters warning against Burr. The New Yorkers had known each other for more than a decade—as political foes and as fellow lawyers. All through that time, Hamilton had nursed his distrust of Burr; now his letters overflowed with angry desperation. As he wrote to South Carolinian John Rutledge Jr. on January 4, 1801,

> As long as the Federal party preserve their high ground of integrity and principle, I shall not despair of the pub-
> lic weal. But if they quit it and descend to be the willing instruments of the Elevation of the most unfit and most dangerous man of the Community to the highest station in the Government—I shall no longer see any anchor for the hopes of good men.

While Hamilton stewed in New York, Jefferson presided over the sessions of the lame-duck Senate in Washington and waited for the House's decision. He kept up an outward show of calm, but privately he seethed at what he saw as Burr's treachery. Madison worked behind the scenes to keep the Republicans together and at least once lost his temper at the idea that Burr should dare to challenge Jefferson. Other Republicans, such as Governor James Monroe of Virginia, warned that they would not tolerate a Burr victory. Some observers began to fret about the chances of civil war should the House throw the election to Burr. Burr still insisted that he was willing to defer to Jefferson and that in his view

Jefferson should be elected, but Jefferson and his backers did not believe Burr, distrusting him as much as Hamilton did.

The controversy swirling around the electoral deadlock made Burr's character as a public man and political leader a pivotal issue. On the surface, it seemed that Burr was at least as worthy a candidate as his rival. Born in 1756, the son and grandson of Calvinist ministers (his mother's father was the great theologian Jonathan Edwards), Burr attended the College of New Jersey at Princeton, beginning his studies as Madison was finishing his. At the start of the Revolution, he enlisted in the Continental Army, distinguishing himself for valor in the failed American invasion of Canada. Assigned to General Washington's staff in the fall of 1776, he lasted two stormy weeks, for he did not think much of the commander in chief and he wanted to get training in strategy and tactics, not to draft and copy letters and memoranda. Transferring to General Israel Putnam's staff, Burr was assigned the task of leading Continental forces against Loyalist units in upper New Jersey and New York. In this grueling campaign, Burr distinguished himself again for courage and command.

After resigning his commission due to ill health, Burr won admission to the New York bar and built a thriving law practice. He also married a woman a few years older than himself, the widow of a British officer; they had one daughter, named Theodosia after her mother, who died soon afterward. Although Burr did not play a leading role in the argument over the Constitution in 1787–88, he emerged as a major Republican power in 1791, winning a seat in the U.S. Senate from Hamilton's father-in-law, Philip Schuyler. Defeated in 1797 in his bid for reelection, Burr served briefly as New York's attorney general and made no secret of his hopes for higher office.

Despite his record of public service and personal bravery, many of Burr's contemporaries had doubts about him. Unlike Adams, Jefferson, Madison, or Hamilton, he had almost no interest in political or constitutional principles. Burr's supporters, arguing that this lack was a virtue, painted him as a calm, detached observer who was not a prisoner of theoretical schemes. His foes, charging that he stood for no principle at all, whispered that he wanted to be a second Napoleon or Caesar. Burr's private life also gave rise to rumors about his fitness for office. Not only was he infamous as a ladies' man, he also was as generous and irresponsible with his money as any Virginia gentleman planter could be, and a land-speculation scandal had tainted his service as attorney general.

Choosing between Jefferson and Burr left a group of moderate Federalist representatives wrestling with their consciences. They had flirted with the idea of supporting Burr in the hope of winning a role in his administration; but, as a sense of crisis enveloped the nation, they had second thoughts. Finally, they decided that backing Burr was not worth the risk to the Constitution or the Union. Even so, they could not bring themselves to vote for Jefferson. Led by Delaware's James A. Bayard, they hit on a scheme that would help them to break the deadlock while saving face.

On February 17, 1801, on the thirty-sixth ballot, Federalists from Delaware, South Carolina, Vermont, and Maryland cast blank ballots. In effect, they abstained from the election, allowing a majority of the state delegations in the House that actually cast votes to choose Jefferson, satisfying the Constitution's requirements. Three days later, a committee of senators and representatives informed Jefferson formally of his election; his gracious, brief acceptance speech suggests his relief at the end of the electoral deadlock.

At the same time that Bayard and his colleagues agreed on their strategy to break the deadlock in the House, Bayard tried to get something in return from Jefferson—a commitment to embrace certain Federalist policies as the price for resolving the electoral crisis. For more than a century after the election of 1800, Bayard and his descendants insisted that

Jefferson had made such commitments, but Jefferson and those taking his part rejected these claims.

Thereafter, politicians wrestled with the challenge of amending the Constitution to prevent another such contested election. Indeed, Alexander Hamilton was one of the first to hit upon the obvious solution, but it took nearly four years for Congress to agree to it. Proposed in 1803 and ratified in time for the 1804 Presidential election, the 12th Amendment directed Presidential electors to cast separate ballots for President and Vice President. In the process, this amendment doomed the Federalists, which is why so many New England Federalists fought so hard against it.

Larger political forces had reduced the Federalists to a party with political power only in New England, crippling whatever chance they had to win the Presidency. Under the original electoral college, their best chance was to throw a disputed election into the House, where they might bargain with the ultimate winner for power and influence. The 12th Amendment foreclosed that possibility once and for all.

Despite the agonies of the electoral-college deadlock of 1800–1801, the election of 1800 was a landmark in not just American history but world history. It marked the first peacetime transfer of power in a republic from one "party" to another. Such leading moderate Federalists as outgoing President John Adams and the new chief justice of the United States, John Marshall of Virginia, deserve much of the credit for this achievement, for both men worked hard for a peaceful transition from a Federalist to a Republican administration. Unfortunately, Adams was embittered by his defeat at the polls, angered at what he saw as Jefferson's wild and impractical political ideas, and tormented by private sorrow. In December 1800, his son Charles Adams, struggling with alcoholism, had died at the age of 30, soon after he had lost a large sum of money entrusted to him by his oldest brother, John Quincy Adams; the death was either an accidental drowning or a suicide.

Seeking to preserve some toehold in the government for the Federalists, Adams took advantage of the last major enactment by the lame-duck Federalist Congress, the Judiciary Act of 1801. This law created a new set of federal appellate courts and other judicial offices—reforms long sought by justices of the Supreme Court and the legal profession. Thus, Adams set out to improve the federal bench and to salvage something for the defeated Federalists. He named loyal Federalists to these new judgeships, and the Senate swiftly confirmed them. Adams's enemies claimed—wrongly—that the President had stayed up after midnight on his last day in office, signing official certificates (judicial commissions) for the "midnight judges."

Adams and Jefferson met a few times in early 1801, but their discussions did nothing to relieve the strained feelings between them. Furthermore, Adams's wounded spirit, and his sorrow at his son's tragic death, left him with no desire to attend Jefferson's inauguration. At 4:00 on the morning of March 4, 1801, he climbed into a carriage and left Washington, D.C., for the long, sad trip back to Massachusetts. For years afterward, he and his wife, Abigail—in many ways a more vigorous and partisan politician than he was—nursed their hurt feelings against Jefferson and mourned the loss of the man who had once been their closest friend.

8

"WE ARE ALL REPUBLICANS, WE ARE ALL FEDERALISTS" (1801–1805)

On the morning of March 4, 1801, Thomas Jefferson arose in the Conrad and McMunn boarding house, in Washington, D.C., where he had stayed while he was Vice President, dressed with understated care, and walked, with a crowd of friends and supporters, to the still-unfinished Capitol building. In the Senate Chamber, he took the oath of office from Chief Justice John Marshall, becoming the third President of the United States and the first to be inaugurated in the nation's permanent capital. Flanked by Marshall and Vice President Aaron Burr, Jefferson turned to face the assembled members of Congress and a crowd of more than 1,000 onlookers, and began his inaugural address. His audience was disappointed, for, as the hostess and political observer Margaret Bayard Smith recorded in her journal, his trembling voice barely carried past the first few rows of the chamber. When Americans read his speech in the newspapers, however, they found a moving testament of democratic faith.

Jefferson stressed that liberty—in particular, the people's liberty to criticize their government—helped to make the government of the United States "the strongest on earth." He also insisted that "we are all republicans, we are all federalists," by which he meant that all Americans rejected monarchy and embraced republican government, and that all Americans agreed that the powers of government were well divided between the federal government and the states. Finally, he reaffirmed his commitment to "a wise and frugal government" that would have friendly relations with all nations but "entangling alliances with none." With these statements, he declared his purpose to interpret the Constitution narrowly and strictly, to rein in the powers of the general government, and to avoid the dangers of being pulled into European wars.

After his inauguration, there were no festive dinners or balls; Jefferson rejected such celebrations because they clashed with the simple republican manners that he wanted his new administration to display. According to popular legend, he walked back to his boarding house and stood with the other boarders, awaiting his chance to sit and have dinner. Only two weeks later did he move to the large, drafty Executive Mansion, now known as the White House.

Jefferson hailed his victory as "the Revolution of 1800," a triumph that guaranteed the success of the American Revolution. He argued that, by electing him President, the voters had rejected their government's drift into the dangerous paths of centralization, monarchy, aristocracy, British influence, and corruption; instead, they had endorsed his plan to return the nation and its government to a course that would be true to the Revolution's principles and the character of the American people. Jefferson promised that he would make good the promise of both revolutions—of 1776 and of 1800. On March 6, 1801, two days after his inauguration, he wrote to a fellow veteran of the Second Continental Congress, John Dickinson of Delaware:

> The storm through which we have passed, has been tremendous indeed. The tough sides of our Argosie have been thoroughly tried. Her strength has stood the waves into which she was steered, with a view to sink her. We shall put her on her republican tack, & she will now show by the beauty of her motion the skill of her builders.

"EVERY DIFFERENCE OF OPINION IS NOT A DIFFERENCE OF PRINCIPLE"

In one of the most eloquent inaugural addresses in American history, delivered on March 4, 1801, President Thomas Jefferson tried to set the tone for his first term in office. His contemporaries and later generations have admired it as a powerful testimonial to his faith in democracy.

Every difference of opinion is not a difference of principle. We have called by different names brethren of the same principle. We are all republicans, we are all federalists. If there by any among us who would wish to dissolve this Union or to change its republican form, let them stand undisturbed as monuments of the safety with which error of opinion may be tolerated where reason is left free to combat it. I know, indeed, that some honest men fear that a republican government can not be strong, that this government is not strong enough; but would the honest patriot, in the full tide of successful experiment, abandon a government which has so far kept us free and firm on the theoretic and visionary fear that this government, the world's best hope, may by possibility want energy to preserve itself? I trust not. I believe this, on the contrary, the strongest government on earth. I believe it the only one where very man, at the call of the law, would fly to the standard of the law, and would meet invasions of the public order as his own personal concern. Sometimes it is said that man can not be trusted with the government of himself. Can he then be trusted with the government of others? Or have we found angels in the forms of kings to govern him? Let history answer this question.

Assuring Dickinson that his election meant the revival of the idea that human beings could govern themselves, Jefferson predicted that other nations would emulate the American example, bringing happiness to a large, increasing proportion of the world.

Jefferson based his Presidency on a few key principles. He tried to eliminate from the government every trace of monarchical or aristocratic customs and Hamilton's fiscal policies, specifically, the national debt, a standing army, and a powerful navy. And he was committed to rid the federal judiciary of Federalists who, he was convinced, would use their powers to undermine the Jeffersonian Republican program. Further, he chose candidates for federal executive posts to highlight his commitment to Republican values. This commitment had its limits, however; when in 1807 Secretary of the Treasury Albert Gallatin suggested that Jefferson name women to federal office, the President replied coldly, "The appointment of a woman to office is an innovation for which the public is not prepared, nor am I."

To set the tone for his administration, Jefferson perfected a new kind of Presidential leadership. No orator, he preferred to conduct politics in intimate circles of friends. Building on his own inclinations and on lessons he learned from observing George Washington, he guided his Presidency by two principles: partnership with his cabinet and collaboration with leaders of the Republican majorities in the House and the Senate. His goal was to make his administration a model of cordial relations between the executive and legislative branches of government.

Jefferson also used his extraordinary gifts as a writer to set the agenda of American public life—in his inaugural address, in messages to Congress, and in skillfully crafted public letters on vital national issues. In one such public letter, written on January 1, 1802, to the Baptist Association of Danbury, Connecticut, he rebuked those Federalists who had attacked him as hostile to religion and he declared his support for what he thought the Constitution commanded, strict separation of church and state. This letter was part of Jefferson's campaign to present himself as no foe of religion while attacking the idea that church and state should form an alliance.

On the day he sent this letter, which his advisers reviewed line by line, Jefferson welcomed the famed Baptist preacher, John Leland of Massachusetts, to the nation's capital. Leland brought with him a remarkable gift—a 1,235-pound cheddar cheese (with three smaller cheeses, each seventy pounds) made by his fellow Baptists. Leland had brought the cheeses, with great effort, from Cheshire, Massachusetts, in a cart drawn by six horses and bearing a sign: "THE GREATEST CHEESE IN AMERICA FOR THE GREATEST MAN IN AMERICA." Jefferson paid Leland $200 for the cheeses, so that nobody could accuse him of accepting gifts from poor New England farmers. (In 1805, Federalist Senator William Plumer of New Hampshire recorded in his diary that Jefferson served him some of the famous cheese, which he noted was "very far from being good.") Two days later, Jefferson attended a Baptist service that Leland led in the chamber of the House of Representatives.

Stung nonetheless by Federalist charges that he was an atheist and an enemy to all religion, Jefferson combined his private interest in religion with a political purpose. One inspiration of his religious studies was the Reverend Joseph Priestley, the English liberal theologian most famous for his chemical researches, including his discovery of oxygen. A warm friend to the United States and the French Revolution, Priestley had fled his home city of Birmingham, England, to escape mobs secretly backed by the British government. He settled in western Pennsylvania, where he carried on scientific experiments and wrote extensively about the early history of Christianity. His central goal was to recover Jesus' words and teachings, stripping away centuries of myth and superstition—the handiwork, he argued, of clergymen and theologians. Jefferson decided that he would prepare a small volume

"A WALL OF SEPARATION"

In this letter, written to the Danbury Baptist Association on January 1, 1802, in answer to its appeal for his political backing, Jefferson tried to set the record straight on his views on religion and separation of church and state. He challenged Federalists who insisted on an alliance between organized religion and government, and insisted that the 1st Amendment built "a wall of separation between church and state."

Gentlemen,—The affectionate sentiments of esteem and approbation which you are so good as to express towards me, on behalf of the Danbury Baptist Association, give me the highest satisfaction. My duties dictate a faithful and zealous pursuit of the interests of my constituents, and in proportion as they are persuaded of my fidelity to those duties, the discharge of them becomes more and more pleasing.

Believing with you that religion is a matter which lies solely between man and his God, that he owes account to none other for his faith or his worship, that the legislative powers of government reach actions only, and not opinions, I contemplate with sovereign reverence the act of the whole American people which declared that their legislature should "make no law respecting an establishment of religion, or prohibiting the free exercise thereof," thus building a wall of separation between church and state. Adhering to this expression of the supreme will of the nation in behalf of the rights of conscience, I shall see with sincere satisfaction the progress of those sentiments which tend to restore to man all his natural rights, convinced he has no natural rights in opposition to his social duties.

I reciprocate your kind prayers for the protection and blessing of the common Father and Creator of man, and tender you for yourselves and your religious association, assurances of my high respect and esteem.

distilling the essence of the Four Gospels and that he would package it as an attack on the superstitions of the Federalists.

On April 21, 1803, Jefferson wrote to his friend, and fellow signer of the Declaration, Dr. Benjamin Rush of his admiration of Priestley's work, explaining, "To the corruptions of Christianity, I am indeed opposed; but not to the genuine precepts of Jesus himself. I am a Christian, in the only sense in which he wished any one to be; sincerely attached to his doctrines, in preference to all others; ascribing to himself every human excellence, & believing he never claimed any other." In 1804, he prepared a manuscript that he called "The Philosophy of Jesus," with the cutting subtitle, "for the use of the Indians unembarrassed with matters of fact or faith beyond the level of their comprehension." The "Indians" whom he had in mind were not Native Americans but rather the Federalists. Jefferson put the manuscript aside and never published it, and it was later lost; not until 1983 was a scholarly reconstruction of it published as part of *The Papers of Thomas Jefferson*.

In other aspects of his Presidency, Jefferson was determined to display his attachment to Republican habits. For example, he refused to appear before a joint session of Congress to deliver the State of the Union address as a speech, because such ceremonies echoed the way that British monarchs opened Parliament. (His decision also conveniently fit with his dislike for public speaking.) Instead, he sent a written message that a clerk read to the senators and representatives, setting a precedent that lasted for more than a century. He also reshaped other ways of doing Presidential business to express republican principles. The Executive Mansion became something of a national museum, in which Jefferson exhibited natural history specimens; in his office, he kept his pet mockingbird, Dick, who usually stayed in his cage, though sometimes Jefferson allowed him to fly around the room.

When, in 1803, the new British minister to the United States, Sir Anthony Merry, was presented to the President, he arrived at the Executive Mansion in full diplomatic regalia, complete with ceremonial sword, as was the custom in Europe. To his shock, Jefferson received him wearing casual clothing, including a dressing-gown and a pair of worn-out carpet slippers. Also, Merry complained, Jefferson had no respect for social rank. Instead of seating guests at state dinners according to rank, as defined by Old World standards of protocol, Jefferson decreed that everyone could sit where he or she wished. This system of seating, which Jefferson called by the French phrase pele-mele, resembled a game of musical chairs; those not deft enough to grab the seats they desired either had to sit at the end of the table or had to stand, uncomfortably juggling plates and cups.

European diplomats mocked the President's republican etiquette, but they admitted that he was a master of diplomacy. Keenly aware that the United States was a new, fragile member of the community of nations, Jefferson charted a careful course in foreign policy. He sought to steer the United States away from unnecessary conflicts with European powers, in particular, to keep from being sucked into the wars between Napoleon's French Empire and the rest of Europe. At the same time, Jefferson was eager and willing to defend American interests, even if it meant risking conflict with Spain or France. This readiness was the source of his most important foreign-policy achievement, the Louisiana Purchase of 1803.

Jefferson knew that Spain's control of the lower Mississippi River and the port of New Orleans threatened American settlements in the lower South, mainly by threatening to induce them to leave the Union and become separate states under the sway of Spain. He therefore decided to assert American power in the region, hoping to pressure Spain to give up its North American colonies. Thus, he began to plan an expedition to explore the heart of the North American continent, both American and foreign territory alike, to be led by his secretary, Meriwether Lewis, a captain in the United States Army. He devised this expedition as one of scientific investigation, seeking to amass knowledge of the natural world. At the same time, it would assert American power, in particular, the nation's claim to the continent's interior.

As Jefferson was planning this venture, he learned that France had taken over Spain's American colonies, including the Louisiana Territory and New Orleans. He therefore named a valued political ally, Robert R. Livingston of New York, to go to France to persuade Napoleon Bonaparte, then First Consul of the French Republic, to sell New Orleans to the United States. At first, Napoleon and his foreign minister, Talleyrand (a key figure in the XYZ Affair of 1798), rebuffed Livingston; in response, Jefferson sent James Monroe to aid the New Yorker. Meanwhile, Napoleon and Talleyrand reconsidered. Aware that Louisiana was draining his finances, Napoleon wanted to unload it for ready cash. Talleyrand agreed, believing that France should concentrate on Europe. Days before Monroe arrived, the French offered the startled Livingston a magnificent deal: not just New Orleans but the whole Louisiana Territory, for 15 million dollars, or less than four cents per acre.

When President Jefferson and Secretary of State Madison learned of the proposal, they were astonished, delighted—and nervous. Was the treaty constitutional? Jefferson scoured the Constitution but could find no provision that, he thought, would allow the federal government to make treaties to buy land or to spend money to buy land; he even drafted a proposed constitutional amendment authorizing such measures. As he explained on September 7, 1803, to Senator Wilson Cary Nicholas of Virginia,

> When an instrument admits two constructions, the one safe, the other dangerous, the one precise, the other indefinite, I prefer that which is safe & precise. I had rather ask an enlargement of power from the nation, where it is found necessary, than to assume it by a con-

struction which would make our powers boundless. Our peculiar security is in possession of a written constitution. Let us not make it a blank paper by construction.... Let us go on then perfecting it, by adding, by way of amendment to the Constitution, those powers which time & trial show are still wanting.

Ultimately, however, Jefferson decided that the deal offered by France was so valuable that no one would challenge the treaty's constitutionality, and set aside the amendment proposal as unnecessary for the present. He persuaded himself that, if necessary, Congress would be free to propose such an amendment to confer the blessing of constitutionality on the treaty after the fact. On April 28, 1803, the French and the Americans signed the three treaties making up the Louisiana Purchase. The Senate soon ratified them, though Federalists mocked Jefferson for having abandoned strict interpretation of the Constitution.

Meanwhile, Jefferson returned to planning the expedition to be led by Captain Lewis and Lieutenant William Clark. Its first priority would be to find and map a westward route to the Pacific—the Northwest Passage sought by Europeans and Americans for 300 years. With this end in view, and drawing on his extensive reading and research on the history

This elkskin-bound notebook is one of many used by Lewis and Clark to keep journals of their expedition. Jefferson supervised Lewis's training in a wide range of scientific and technical subjects to prepare him to lead the expedition.

of exploration, he framed a set of instructions for Lewis. He then showed this draft to the members of his cabinet. For once, Madison had little or nothing to contribute. By contrast, the shrewd, astute Levi Lincoln, Jefferson's attorney general and a superb politician, warned that there might be no Northwest Passage for the expedition to find, which would make the expedition an expensive laughingstock.

Lincoln urged Jefferson to establish a list of goals that the explorers could meet, even if they failed in their central purpose. Jefferson agreed, reshaping his draft according to Lincoln's advice. His confidential letter to Lewis, dated June 20, 1803, became the expedition's charter and set the standard for all later government efforts to explore the natural world. Besides seeking a Northwest Passage, Lewis and Clark were to map the continent's interior, to assess its plant and animal life and natural resources, and to establish diplomatic and trade relationships with Native American nations. In these efforts, Lewis, Clark, and their "Corps of Discovery" were heroically successful. They sent many specimens of plant and animal life back east, along with journals and extensive lists of vocabularies of Native American languages. Also, they persuaded Native American nations to send diplomatic missions to "the Great Father" in Washington, D.C.

As Lewis and Clark headed westward, they discovered that the land grew more rugged, with vast, towering mountain ranges, wide stretches of desert, and turbulent, rushing rivers that even light canoes could not travel. They also learned that North America was wider than anyone had believed or expected. Though they reached the Pacific Ocean in 1805, on their return a year later they had to report to the disappointed Jefferson that the fabled Northwest Passage did not exist. He delighted, however, in their amazingly rich reports, travel journals, and samples of plant and animal life. In many ways, Jefferson also was an explorer of the American West, a full partner in the historic success of the Lewis and Clark Expedition.

Jefferson, Lewis, and Clark made assumptions that said a great deal about their view of Native Americans. The explorers presented peace medallions to leaders of these nations, and they—and Jefferson—assumed that any leader who accepted a medallion accepted the ultimate political power of "the Great Father" (the term that Presidents Washington, Adams, and Jefferson had used to describe themselves in messages to Native American nations). They were wrong, for most Native American leaders saw themselves as equals of the U.S. President and understood gifts of medallions as the usual exchanges of presents between equal parties in diplomatic negotiations. Also, the delegations who came east to visit President Jefferson did not come to bow to his authority. Rather, they demanded trading goods and insisted on negotiating trading treaties as equals. These misunderstandings between Jefferson, Lewis, and Clark, on the one hand, and leaders of Native American nations, on the other hand, foretold generations of similar conflicts between whites and Native Americans.

Meriwether Lewis and William Clark gave medals bearing a portrait of Jefferson to Native American chiefs during their famed expedition to explore the territories acquired under the Louisiana Purchase.

The Jefferson administration continued to seek friendly relations with Native American peoples, but it based its seemingly enlightened policy on assumptions that, viewed today, are highly troubling. Jefferson urged his countrymen to abandon their hostility to Native Americans, but he also hoped to reshape Native American societies so that they would fit more comfortably within his expanding "empire for liberty." Setting aside his commitment to strict separation of church and state, he sent Christian missionaries to establish schools in western territories to educate

Native Americans—and convert them to Christianity. He also tried to persuade Native American peoples to adopt European and American ideas of ownership of land and an economy based on individual farming, and thus to abandon their cultures based on hunting, gathering, and communal agriculture. Another change that Jefferson urged on them was that men should take on the tasks of agriculture, which traditionally had been the province of women. If they adopted this new way of life, they could unite with their white neighbors and build together a new society devoted to liberty and peace. If they clung to their old ways, Jefferson warned, they would be overwhelmed by the expansion of the white American republic and "disappear from the earth."

Jefferson faced another significant foreign-policy challenge in his first term, one that had vexed him from his first days as a diplomat. For decades, Barbary corsairs—ships of the Muslim peoples living on North Africa's Barbary Coast (Tunis, Algiers, Morocco, and Tripoli)—ruled the Mediterranean Sea, demanding that other nations pay tribute to them as the price of leaving their shipping alone. Often, these "Barbary pirates" would seize a merchant ship and hold its cargo and its crew and passengers for ransom. Before 1776, American ships had been under the British Royal Navy's protection. With the coming of independence, however, American vessels were on their own, and often fell prey to the Barbary corsairs.

Through the 1780s, Jefferson received pitiful appeals from American prisoners held hostage in North Africa, but the United States had no money to ransom them. Frustrated, Jefferson demanded an international alliance to wage war on the Barbary pirates, but the United States lacked the money and resources to fight a naval war, and the other nations that Jefferson wanted to take part did not believe that the alliance would work.

Jefferson remained determined to end the Barbary states' attacks on American shipping. In 1801, the President rejected a demand by the pasha of Tripoli (today the capital of Libya) that the United States pay $225,000 in tribute, with further payments of $25,000 per year. Insulted, the pasha declared war, and Jefferson sent a small fleet of ships to the Mediterranean. The American fleet intimidated Tunis and Algiers, which broke their alliance with Tripoli. In 1803, however, Tripoli captured the U.S. frigate *Philadelphia* and took its captain and crew hostage. Despite this embarrassing setback, Jefferson held firm. In 1803–4, he sent a new expedition; its leader, Commodore Edward Preble, forced Morocco to make peace with the United States and subjected Tripoli to five separate naval bombardments.

In 1805, Commodore John Rogers and Captain William Eaton led a daring land-and-sea raid on Tripoli, burned the captured *Philadelphia,* rescued its captain and crew, and threatened to seize Tripoli and topple the pasha from his throne. Finally, the pasha and the United States signed a treaty under which the United States paid $60,000 ransom for each American sailor that the dey (ruler) of Algiers held hostage. (In 1815, after a further decade of intermittent conflict, American naval power and diplomacy finally forced the Barbary states to give up their demands for tribute.) Through these events, Jefferson was committed to a broad interpretation of the President's war powers—acting on his own initiative without asking Congress for a declaration of war.

Another foreign-policy problem confronted Jefferson virtually on America's doorstep. France had long held the island of St. Domingue (now known as Hispaniola) in the Caribbean as a colony; in 1791, the enslaved Africans living there, inspired by the French Revolution, revolted against French rule. By 1801, led by Toussaint Louverture, they founded the Republic of Haiti. Viewing these developments warily, Jefferson thought that the island might be a good place to send African-American freed slaves and criminals; he also believed that, if the French were distracted enough by Haiti, they would abandon their colonial holdings on the

Jefferson used his
Presidential war powers
to combat the Barbary
pirates' attacks on
American ships. In
1803, during an
operation ordered by
the President, the
Philadelphia ran
aground and was cap-
tured. The next year
Lieutenant Stephen
Decatur led a daring
raid to rescue its
captain and crew.

North American mainland. And yet he worried that Haiti's existence as a free black republic might spur American slave revolts. Thus, he did not welcome the Haitians' final victory in 1804; rather, he refused to recognize the new republic, and he and his allies quietly supported Southern states in tightening their slavery laws and taking harsher measures to prevent slave uprisings that, he and they feared, might draw inspiration from the Haitian example.

Despite his general commitment to a narrow interpretation of the Constitution, Jefferson wielded executive power with vigor and skill; his first term's greatest achievements showed his willingness to test the constitutional limits of Presidential power. In sending a naval expedition to punish the Barbary Pirates, or acquiring from France the port of New Orleans and the territory of Louisiana, or planning the Lewis and Clark Expedition to explore those western territories, Jefferson showed himself to be a versatile, adaptable chief executive.

In two key ways, the American people's reactions to Jefferson's Presidency gave him reason to believe that he had changed the course of American public life, in a direction that the people welcomed. First, during and after his Presidency, Jefferson received hundreds of letters from ordinary Americans, some praising his policies, some begging for help, some proposing schemes—whether shrewd or daft—for inventions or for public policy, and many simply venting their feelings. He also became a lightning rod for anger, ridicule, and even death threats; one anonymous writer spluttered, "Thomas Jefferson. You are the damdest fool that God put life into. God dam you."

Apparently, Jefferson was the first President to become such a focus of popular attention; comparatively few Americans had written so often or so personally to George Washington or John Adams during their Presidencies. He calmly docketed all these letters among his papers, and tried to answer all the reasonable ones. Second, Americans began to show an interest in acquiring images of their President. In this period, most Americans never got a chance to see the face of their President, nor even one of the various life portraits of Washington, Adams, or Jefferson. Beginning with Jefferson, engravers and printers turned out a profusion of such images for an increasingly eager market.

Despite his widespread popularity, Jefferson ended his first term in office with two major frustrations. The first had to do with public finance. Jefferson had sought to overturn Hamilton's fiscal policies and, as he had promised in his first inaugural address, to create a "wise and frugal" government free of national debt. On January 18, 1802, he complained bitterly to his friend Pierre S. du Pont de Nemours:

> When this government was first established, it was possible to have kept it going on true principles, but the contracted, English, half-lettered ideas of Hamilton, destroyed that hope in the bud. We can pay off his debt in 15. years; but we can never get rid of his financial system. It mortifies me to be strengthening principles which I deem radically vicious, but this vice is entailed on us by the first error.

Even so, Swiss-born Secretary of the Treasury Albert Gallatin struggled to cut the national debt, reducing government spending and promoting sales of western public lands. The brilliant, energetic Gallatin found the money to finance the Louisiana Purchase, to outfit and support the Lewis and Clark Expedition, and to combat the Barbary pirates. When he retired from the Treasury in 1814, five years after Jefferson left the Presidency, Gallatin had reduced the nation's public debt from $80 million (its level in 1801) to $45 million. But Jefferson had wanted to erase Hamilton's fiscal legacy, and that Gallatin could not do.

Jefferson's second frustration, and the greatest defeat of his first term in office, was the failure of his campaign against the federal judiciary. Federalists appointed by Washington and Adams dominated the federal courts, to Jefferson's anger and distrust. He resented the Judiciary Act of 1801, which the lame-duck Federalist Congress and President Adams had used to staff new federal courts with loyal Federalists. Although the law's backers explained that these courts were intended to ease the judiciary's workload, Jefferson saw these Federalist judges as foes of republicanism and hoped to remove them.

The battle began with a discovery of abandoned papers. In March of 1801, when John Marshall stepped down as secretary of state and took up his duties as chief justice, he left at the State Department a pile of judicial commissions— certificates signed by the President and confirmed by the secretary of state indicating that the person named in the commission has been officially named to a federal office. Marshall had run out of time to deliver these commissions, which were for judicial appointments under the 1801 Judiciary Act. Without one's commission, one could not begin service as a judge.

Secretary of State Madison discovered the pile of papers in his new office and discussed them with President Jefferson; the two men agreed that Madison would not deliver the remaining commissions. William Marbury, a Federalist enraged that he could not begin his new job as a justice of the peace of the District of Columbia (and thus could not get his salary), sued Madison for his commission. Not wanting to waste time climbing the federal judicial ladder, Marbury began his lawsuit at the top, in the United States Supreme Court, rather than in a federal trial court. Marbury asked the Court to issue what lawyers call a writ of mandamus—an order that a government official do his duty. In effect, he demanded that the Supreme Court order Madison to give Marbury his commission.

Marshall faced a seeming no-win situation, born of his failure to deliver the commissions. If he issued the writ, he knew that Madison would ignore it, and he had no way to make Madison obey it, for federal courts rely on the executive branch to enforce their orders, and Jefferson's administration would refuse to enforce Marshall's writ. Thus, Jefferson's administration would win. If he did not issue the writ, his failure would make him look weak, and Jefferson's administration also would win. At the same time, the Republican-dominated Congress repealed the 1801 Judiciary Act and canceled the Supreme Court's August 1802 session, keeping the Court from meeting until February 1803, to delay whatever decision Marshall's Court might reach.

On February 24, 1803, when Marshall delivered his opinion for the Court in *Marbury* v. *Madison,* he astonished everyone by finding a way out of the trap. He began by asking whether Marbury had a right to his commission. Answering "Yes," he lectured the Jefferson administration about the rule of law and scolded Madison for not having done his job (delivering Marbury's commission). He next asked if the remedy that Marbury sought—a writ of mandamus—would achieve what Marbury wanted, and again answered "Yes," with another lecture.

But, he then asked, was the remedy a writ of mandamus issued by the Supreme Court in this case? He looked for a statute authorizing the Court to act in this kind of case, and found a section of the Judiciary Act of 1789. He interpreted that statute to give the Court the power to take cases seeking

In 1801, William Marbury filed suit in the U.S. Supreme Court against Secretary of State James Madison, demanding that Madison deliver his commission of office to him. The court issued this "show-cause order" to Madison, demanding that he explain why he had not delivered Marbury's commission. In 1898, a fire in the Capitol partly burned the document.

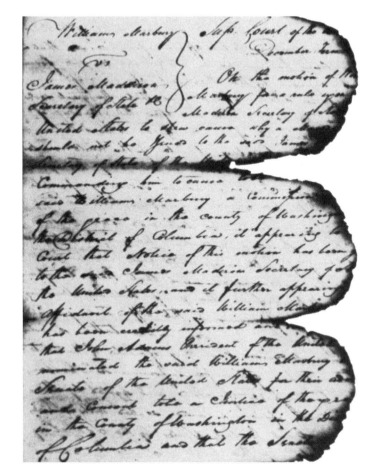

such writs as part of its "original jurisdiction"—the category of cases that can be filed in the Supreme Court first, without having to start in a lower court. But, Marshall noted, the Constitution defines and limits the kinds of cases making up the Court's original jurisdiction. The 1789 statute appeared to expand that set of cases, and thus to collide with the Constitution. Should the Court follow the Constitution or the statute? Marshall drew on Hamilton's argument in *The Federalist No. 78* to show that, whenever a statute contradicts the Constitution, the Court must follow the Constitution and declare that statute unconstitutional.

Judicial review—a court's ability to strike down a statute as unconstitutional—is the Court's most important power.

Thus, in *Marbury,* Marshall asserted and justified a vital, versatile power for the Court. In a neat trick, Marshall reversed the order in which a judge would usually write an opinion, so that he could confront the case on its merits and seize the chance to claim judicial review. If he had followed the normal line of reasoning, beginning by ruling that Marbury had begun his lawsuit in the wrong court, and then dismissing Marbury's lawsuit on that basis, he could not win the great prize of judicial review, and he also would run the risk that Marbury would relaunch the case in the right court and it would reach the Supreme Court again on appeal.

In an even neater trick, Marshall declared unconstitutional a statute that seemed to give the Court more power than the Constitution gave the Court. By rejecting the power that an unconstitutional statute conferred on the Court, Marshall gave the Court vast constitutional power, winning for the Court a role as an authoritative interpreter of the Constitution. The Marshall Court then announced its decision in another, highly technical case, at the same time as *Marbury.* In *Stuart* v. *Laird,* the Court, in an opinion by Associate Justice William Paterson, upheld the 1802 Judiciary Act, which repealed the 1801 act and abolished the new federal courts that the 1801 act had created. Finally, in the neatest trick of all, Marshall not only salvaged a messy situation but left Jefferson in a position in which he could do nothing about what Marshall and the Court had done.

Jefferson was furious, but not at the Court's claim of judicial review. Rather, he seethed at Marshall's lectures to his administration about its duty to follow the law. Furthermore, he and his allies were sure that Marshall and other Federalist judges would use their powers to frustrate Republican policies. Besides, Republicans wanted to achieve two linked goals: to punish Federalist judges for having used the Sedition Act against Republican editors, and to staff the federal courts with reliable Republicans. Thus, with Jefferson's blessing, House Republicans prepared to use the Constitution's impeachment process to drive Federalists from the federal bench.

In late 1803, Jefferson's supporters began their campaign. They first targeted Judge John Pickering of the U.S. District Court in New Hampshire. It was not clear whether Pickering, an aged Federalist whose mind had begun to fail, was going senile, drinking himself into imbecility, or both. The problem was that his case did not fit within recognized uses of the impeachment process. Under the Constitution, federal officials, including judges, can be impeached only for "treason, bribery, or other high crimes and misdemeanors." That last category is a term of art covering specific offenses— but not a pattern of what lawyers call "incapacity." Federalists charged that Pickering's impeachment was the first step in an unconstitutional scheme to remove Federalist judges. Republicans brushed the Federalists' charges aside, for they had the votes; the House impeached Pickering, and the Senate tried, convicted, and removed him.

Second on the Republicans' list was Associate Justice Samuel Chase of the U.S. Supreme Court. Republicans had not forgotten Chase's partisan ways while holding circuit courts, in particular his biased conduct of James Thomson Callender's trial for seditious libel. The House impeached Chase almost as swiftly as it had Pickering, and the Senate began his trial. One of the witnesses was Chief Justice Marshall. Because Republicans hinted threateningly that Marshall would be their final target, his nervous discomfort before the Senate was plain to see.

However, the Senate's trial of Chase did not turn out as Jefferson had hoped. For one thing, the House's chief prosecutor, Virginia Representative John Randolph of Roanoke (a distant cousin of Jefferson), injured his case by his increasingly erratic behavior. For another, Chase's defense team, led by Luther Martin, did a brilliant job of exposing the flaws in the case against Chase. But the ultimate obstacle to Chase's conviction and removal from office was Vice

President Aaron Burr. Burr had been frustrated and offended throughout his term. Distrusting him because of his conduct during the electoral deadlock of 1800–1801, the Jeffersonians had frozen him out of the government.

Beginning in 1802, Burr had flirted with joining the Federalists, and they had backed him in New York's 1804 election for governor. In that contest, Hamilton had campaigned vigorously against Burr, and helped cause Burr's humiliating defeat at the polls that spring. Within two months, Burr and Hamilton were tangled in a bitter dispute in which each man felt that his honor was being attacked; the result was a duel fought at Weehawken, New Jersey, on July 11, 1804. Burr mortally wounded Hamilton, who died the next day.

Hamilton's death doomed Burr's political career. Within weeks, grand juries in New York and New Jersey indicted Burr for Hamilton's murder, and the Republicans chose Governor George Clinton of New York to replace him as Jefferson's running mate. However, Burr still was Vice President, and as such had the duty to preside over the Senate's sessions, including impeachment trials. He was determined to perform his last duties as Vice President with honor; if, in the process, he could vex Jefferson, so much the better. He studied how the British House of Lords tried impeachments and mastered the intricate procedures of impeachment; he even had the Senate chamber redecorated to resemble that of the House of Lords.

Presiding over Chase's trial with dignity and fairness, Burr won respect even from his political foes. Most important, Burr established that an impeachment trial is a blend of a political process and a judicial trial, not a naked exercise of political power by a determined majority. This principle has governed all later impeachment trials. Burr's view of impeachment and his conduct of Chase's trial were key factors in the Senate's vote to acquit Chase. This defeat derailed Jefferson's hopes to use impeachment to drive Federalists from the bench; though, at the same time, Jefferson found some comfort in the hope that the impeachment effort might have scared Federalist judges into behaving themselves. At the trial's close, Burr gave his last speech to the Senate, an eloquent tribute to that body as a defender of liberty and republican government that moved his audience to tears. He then left Washington, D.C., and headed for the West, his career in ruins.

Though Jefferson could not oust the Federalists from the bench, he took other steps to reverse the damage done by efforts to enforce the Sedition Act. One of his first acts as President had been to pardon those convicted under that law; he also pledged to repay any fines levied on them. Though he could not punish Federalist judges for their judicial war on Republican editors, he could disclaim their rulings and undo some of the damage they had caused to freedom of the press.

The problem was that Jefferson's pledge entangled him with someone whom he had once found useful but from whom he now wished to keep his distance. James Thomson Callender, who had been jailed longer than any other Republican editor, besieged Jefferson and Madison with letters demanding repayment of the heavy fine that Justice Chase had imposed on him. The U.S. marshal in Richmond, who held Callender's money, was a Federalist who dragged his feet repaying the fine. Jefferson and Madison tried to explain the problem to Callender, who refused to put up with what he saw as stalling. Jefferson, who hated confrontations, had Madison deal with Callender and the marshal; the secretary of state found both tasks unpleasant and difficult.

Had Callender only wanted his fine repaid, the matter might have ended once the marshal forked over the money, but Callender sought more. In his view, he had played a vital role in Jefferson's victory, so he deserved a reward equal to his sacrifices of liberty and money for the cause. He demanded the federal postmastership in Richmond, Virginia, a well-paying job that would reestablish his social and political status. Jefferson and Madison knew that giving Callender the post would be political suicide. He was a difficult man, ready to pick quarrels even with friends; his foes scoffed at him as a man beneath them, goading him into spectacular rages. Further, Richmond was John Marshall's hometown and a stronghold of Federalism; naming Callender postmaster would be like whacking a hornet's nest with a stick.

As Jefferson and Madison ignored Callender's increasingly bitter demands for a suitable reward, he seethed with frustration. His hopes for vindication were dashed, and the delays in repaying his fine made the failure of his bid for office more galling. He decided to seek revenge. Accepting a job as editor of the Richmond *Recorder*, Callender reinvented himself as an impartial journalist who would uncover wrongdoing on all sides. His venomous, jeering articles exposed scandals public and private, injuring friends and foes alike. Although he wrote with appalling viciousness, he tended to get his facts right, which caused his targets all the more pain and embarrassment.

Callender's most famous attack focused on his former hero. On September 1, 1802, he charged that Jefferson, "the man whom the people delight to honor," was having a sexual relationship with one of his slaves—"dusky Sally," soon identified as Sally Hemings. Callender claimed that Jefferson had fathered several children by her, and that one—allegedly named Tom—closely resembled the President. Callender's savage glee in recounting the story had two sources: his anger that Jefferson had forsaken him, and his racist loathing of sexual relations between whites and blacks. After two articles, however, Callender ran out of steam; he had laid all his facts before the public, and nothing had come of it.

Though Federalists spread his charges through New England, most voters dismissed the story as repellent scandal-mongering. Callender himself became a target of ridicule and disbelief; critics used his increasingly serious drinking problem to undermine his credibility as a journalist. On July 17, 1803, after witnesses reported that he had been wandering intoxicated through Richmond's streets, his body was found in a nearby river; he apparently fell in while drunk and drowned. Callender's death ended his efforts to smear Jefferson with charges having to do with Sally Hemings. Even so, Federalists continued to use the Hemings story against the President.

Another charge against Jefferson surfaced at the same time as the Hemings accusation. It is not clear how John Walker finally learned of Jefferson's attempt to seduce his wife in the late 1760s, but, once he did, he was determined "to obtain satisfaction" from the President—forcing Jefferson either to give him an explanation or to fight a duel with him. An embarrassed Jefferson had to write a statement for Walker admitting that as a young, unmarried man, he had attempted to seduce Mrs. Walker and that she had spurned his advances. With this statement, Jefferson preserved the Walkers' honor and shouldered the blame himself.

In the first months of his second term, he still was struggling with problems posed by the Walker affair. On July 1, 1805, he wrote to Secretary of the Navy Robert Smith, "You will perceive that I plead guilty to one of their charges, that when young and single I offered love to a handsome lady. I acknowledge its incorrectness. It is the only one founded in truth among all their allegations against me." For nearly two centuries, Jefferson's defenders have interpreted that passage as his denial that he was sexually intimate with Sally Hemings.

Federalist newspapers kept the Hemings and Walker accusations alive. Frustrated by their defeat at the polls in 1800 and the likelihood that they would lose again in 1804, Federalists used the only weapon they had left—the press. Jefferson officially suffered their attacks in silence, but behind the scenes he encouraged Republican state officials to prosecute Federalist editors in state courts for the common-law crime of seditious libel. He insisted that such prosecutions did not clash with his opposition to the federal Alien and

Sedition Acts, which were barred by the 1st Amendment. Because, as he saw it, the 1st Amendment did not bind state governments, states could prosecute people for seditious libel. In 1804, however, in *People* v. *Croswell,* one of the last cases that Hamilton argued, New York's courts rejected the crime of seditious libel, setting a precedent of national significance.

Also, angered by reports from Connecticut Republicans, such as Postmaster General Gideon Granger, Jefferson encouraged that state's U.S. attorney to prosecute Federalist printers, who had attacked the President as immoral, for seditious libel under a vague doctrine known as the "federal common law." When the printers threatened to introduce at their trials evidence about the Walker affair (to prove their charges that Jefferson was immoral), the President changed his mind and the U.S. Attorney abandoned his plans to prosecute the printers.

Jefferson's first term as President was saddened by the unexpected death, on April 17, 1804, of his younger daughter, Maria Jefferson Eppes (Polly). Hearing the news, Abigail Adams, who in the 1780s had almost been a second mother to Polly, wrote to express her condolences. Mrs. Adams, however, could not forgive or forget the abuse that Jefferson's supporters, particularly Callender, had heaped on her husband. Thus, she signed her letter, "One who once took pleasure in sub-scribing herself your friend. . . ." Ignoring her pointed closing, Jefferson wrote a warm, friendly letter seeking to reopen friendly relations with her and her husband. In reply, Mrs. Adams scolded Jefferson for allowing his backers to attack her husband and for looking the other way while they abused him. In the letters that followed, Jefferson tried to defend himself, but Mrs. Adams had no reluctance to engage in confrontation, and she was more than willing to challenge him with what she saw as differences between his words and his deeds. She closed the correspondence with a blunt reproof, and afterward showed the exchange of letters to her husband, who wrote that he had no comment to make.

9

"A SPLENDID MISERY" (1805–1809)

On May 13, 1797, Thomas Jefferson had written to Elbridge Gerry that he was relieved to have been elected to the Vice Presidency rather than the Presidency: "The second office of this government is honorable & easy, the first is but a splendid misery." His unhappy second term as President showed how difficult and painful he found his tenure as the nation's chief executive. Whereas in his first term he had showed initiative, creativity, and flexibility, regularly seizing opportunities to direct events, in his second term he was, rather, reacting to events, while displaying dogmatism, intolerance, and rigidity.

In 1804, Jefferson and Governor George Clinton of New York easily won that year's Presidential contest, fending off a challenge from the beleaguered Federalists, led by Charles C. Pinckney of South Carolina and Rufus King of New York. At his inauguration, Jefferson delivered an optimistic inaugural address, congratulating the nation on the happy results of his first term's policies and foretelling more good news to come:

> In giving these outlines, I do not mean, fellow citizens, to arrogate to myself the merits of the measures; that is

due, in the first place, to the reflecting character of our citizens at large, who, by the weight of public opinion, influence and strengthen the public measures; it is due to the sound discretion with which they select from among themselves those to whom they confide the legislative duties; it is due to the zeal and wisdom of the characters thus selected, who lay the foundation of public happiness in wholesome laws, the execution of which alone remains for others; and it is due to the able and faithful auxiliaries, whose patriotism has associated with me in the executive functions.

At first, it seemed that his second term would be graced by successes flowing from the policies and initiatives he had launched in his first term. In late 1805, news reached Jefferson of the agreement negotiated between the United States and the pasha of Tripoli under which the pasha promised not to demand any further American tribute, and the United States ransomed the remaining Americans held captive at Tripoli. This report brought a fitting end to Jefferson's efforts to resolve the problems posed by the Barbary pirates. Then, in 1806, Meriwether Lewis and William Clark returned triumphantly, with extensive maps, reports, and plant and animal specimens, capping the labors of the Lewis and Clark Expedition. Jefferson adorned the Executive Mansion and Monticello with choice specimens brought back by the two captains and their Corps of Discovery, and sought to have their findings made available to the world's scientific community.

Soon, however, events at home and abroad cast a cloud over Jefferson's Presidency. In the House of Representatives, the alliance of Republicans began to splinter, as some southern Republicans began to question Jefferson's use of national governmental power. The dissidents' leader was John Randolph of Roanoke, a member of Virginia's most powerful family (and a distant relative of Jefferson). Randolph had backed the Kentucky and Virginia Resolutions of 1798 condemning the Alien and Sedition Acts and had led the

Jeffersonian Republicans' failed impeachment of Justice Samuel Chase. At the same time, Randolph, who chaired the powerful House Committee on Ways and Means, had grown increasingly unhappy with Jefferson's bold experiments with federal constitutional power. He opposed the Louisiana Purchase because, he argued, the Constitution did not give Congress power to make treaties for the purchase of land. This was the same concern that had spurred Jefferson to draft a proposed constitutional amendment, which, to Randolph's ire, he abandoned. Jefferson's other uses of Presidential power to shape American foreign relations also offended Randolph's sense of what the Constitution did and did not permit.

Two major Jeffersonian initiatives in 1806 caused Randolph to reach the breaking point. The first was Jefferson's attempt to end the controversy sparked by the notorious Yazoo land frauds. In 1794, land speculators bribed the Georgia legislature to make them sweeping grants of the state's western lands. When the scandal was revealed, the voters rose in revolt, sweeping a new legislature into power and the old legislature out. The new legislature repealed the land-grant laws and staged a huge ritual burning of the offending statutes in a great bonfire, but the speculators charged that the grants could not be legally repealed. Jefferson proposed that the federal government reimburse the claims of members of the Yazoo Land Company, which Randolph saw as a dangerous interference by the federal government in state affairs. The second critical issue was Jefferson's attempt to persuade Emperor Napoleon I to sell western Florida to the United States, following the precedent of the 1803 Louisiana Purchase. As he had in 1803, Randolph bitterly opposed the 1806 negotiations, because, he insisted, the Constitution nowhere gave the President or the federal government such powers.

By late 1806, Randolph had had enough. He announced that he and several allies from southern states were breaking with Jefferson. Neither Jeffersonian Republicans nor Hamiltonian Federalists, they were a "third something"; Randolph used the Latin phrase *tertium quid*. Their guiding principle, he proclaimed, was states' rights—a cause that Jefferson once championed but now betrayed.

Angered by Randolph's declaration of independence, Jefferson worked with the leaders of the Republican majority in the House to oust him from his chairmanship of the Committee on Ways and Means. Randolph and his allies found that they could not muster enough backing to form a real national political party. All they could do was use oratory and parliamentary procedure to cause unending trouble in the House for Jefferson.

While Jefferson contended with Randolph and the Tertium Quids, he was far more disturbed by the mysterious doings of former Vice President Aaron Burr. In the spring of 1805, disgraced by his killing of Hamilton and his party's abandonment of him, Burr headed west. Nobody, perhaps not even Burr, knew what he had in mind. Probably he was seeking whatever opportunity might turn up to repair his fortunes and rebuild his reputation.

His destination, the lower Mississippi River valley, was a good place to explore his options. Many of the region's settlers had long chafed at the neglect of their interests by a distant federal government and had toyed with breaking away from the Union, either to ally themselves with Spain, Britain, or France, or to go it alone. Foreign agents from the European great powers kept careful watch on the political temper of the Southwest, hoping to exploit the growing atmosphere of discontent and thus to cause trouble for the fragile United States. To make matters worse, General James Wilkinson, commander of American military forces in the region, was secretly pocketing fees from British, Spanish, and—until 1803—French agents, in addition to his federal salary.

Traveling through the region, Burr met with politicians who admired what they called his stalwart defense of his honor in his duel with Hamilton. Many of them poured out their unhappiness with the federal government and grumbled that the region should secede from the Union. Burr nodded, smiled, and listened, but he kept his own counsel. He also supplied guns from his personal stock to the Louisiana militia, which lacked firearms and feared a war with local Native American nations. Finally, he revived his friendship with Wilkinson, whom he had known and liked when the two were officers in the Continental army. Soon Wilkinson was pocketing regular payments from Burr as well.

Several of Burr's allies from New York joined him in the Southwest, and rumors began to reach the government in Washington of various plots in which Burr was supposed to play a key role. In some versions, he was preparing to launch a war to conquer Mexico (still a colony of the dying Spanish empire), either to add to the United States or to establish as his kingdom. Other variants had him scheming to conquer Mexico and the Southwestern states and territories. Jefferson read each report with mounting anger and alarm. He soon came to believe the worst-case scenario—that Burr was scheming to create an empire for himself by conquering Mexico and the southwest United States. Always willing to believe the worst when Burr was involved, on November 26, 1806, Jefferson ordered Burr's arrest on charges of treason.

In late January 1807, federal authorities arrested Burr and hauled him before a federal grand jury in the Mississippi Territory—but were forced to release him for want of evidence. They seized him again on February 19, 1807, near the Tombigbee River in what is now Alabama. On January 22, 1807, before news of Burr's release and re-arrest had reached the capital, Jefferson issued a special message to Congress reporting on the crisis and declaring that the former Vice President's "guilt is placed beyond question." Greeting the news of Burr's arrest with almost hysterical relief, Jefferson worked with George Hay, the U.S. Attorney in Richmond, and others in the federal government to build the case against

Burr. On April 20, 1807, he wrote to his longtime friend and political ally, the Virginia politician William Branch Giles:

> Against Burr, personally, I never had one hostile senti-ment. I never, indeed, thought him an honest, frank-dealing man, but considered him as a crooked gun or other perverted machine whose aim or stroke you could never be sure of. Still, while he possessed the confidence of the nation, I thought it my duty to respect in him their confidence, & to treat him as if he deserved it....

On March 30, 1807, federal marshals brought Burr before the United States 4th Circuit Court, in Richmond, Virginia. There George Hay presented an indictment charging Burr with treason and conspiring to invade a neighboring nation at peace with the United States—that is, Spanish Mexico. In a bitter irony for Jefferson, however, Burr came to trial before precisely the wrong judge for the President's purposes: Chief Justice John Marshall, who was assigned to the 4th Circuit. Jefferson greeted with dismay and anger the news that Marshall would preside over Burr's trial.

Chief Justice John Marshall, a Virginia Federalist, led the Supreme Court from 1801 to 1835. He and Jefferson were distant cousins, but they distrusted and disliked each other. One reason for this shared dislike was Marshall's admiration for and agreement with Alexander Hamilton's interpretations of the Constitution.

The proceedings in *United States* v. *Burr* attracted national attention. A galaxy of leading attorneys flocked to Burr's defense, among them Edmund Randolph, a former governor of Virginia and Jefferson's successor as secretary of state, and Luther Martin, a diehard Federalist politician and former attorney general of Maryland, who had tangled with Jefferson in the controversy over Chief Logan and Captain Cresap. Burr, a superb lawyer himself, played an active role in his own defense. On April 1, 1807, Marshall ruled that Burr could be held for trial on the charge of conspiracy, but he rejected the prosecution's bid to try Burr for treason. With that ruling, the case formally began.

In a startling move, Burr demanded that the court issue a subpoena commanding President Jefferson to appear as a witness and to produce papers from government files that Burr needed for his defense. George Hay declared that Jefferson would refuse to appear. At issue was whether the President should be able to protect the confidentiality of his consultations with members of his administration—an idea known today as executive privilege.

After extensive argument by lawyers on both sides, Chief Justice Marshall granted Burr's motion. He declared that the President, like any other person, was subject to the command of the courts. Neither the Constitution nor the law of evidence contained any exception for the President. Even if, as Jefferson claimed, disclosure of certain documents might harm the public safety (what we call national security), Marshall held that the court had to make that finding by examining the subpoenaed materials in private.

The confrontation between Jefferson and Marshall eased when Burr made clear that he would be happy to get only the records and papers that he had subpoenaed, and neither needed nor wanted to call Jefferson as a witness; in response, the President turned over the documents. The trial, which dominated the month of August, turned into a farce. The chief witness against Burr, General Wilkinson, appeared more deserving of trial than Burr did, and Burr's lawyers scored point after point on such matters as the Constitution's narrow, precise definition of treason, which the federal indictment did not meet.

On September 1, 1807, the jury gave its verdict, finding Burr "not proved to be guilty under this indictment by any evidence submitted to us." In other words, the jurors suspected that Burr had been up to something, but they could not find him guilty on the evidence they had heard. Furious at the outcome, Jefferson denounced the jury and Marshall as biased and irresponsible, but there was nothing he could do. Burr left for Europe, where he fruitlessly sought the support of various nations for unspecified but grand schemes. In 1812, after New York and New Jersey had abandoned their 1804 indictments of him for dueling and murder (growing out of his fatal duel with Hamilton), Burr returned to New York City; he lived quietly there, practicing law, until he died at the age of 80 in 1836.

Jefferson found American foreign policy in his second term even more difficult, frustrating, and dispiriting than his long, inconclusive struggle with Burr. For a decade, wars between Revolutionary France and its neighbors had ravaged Europe. The crowning of Napoleon Bonaparte as emperor had brought a short-lived peace, but Napoleon plunged Europe into further wars. At first, this conflict was good for American interests. For one thing, the Louisiana Purchase of 1803 was the direct result of Napoleon's need to raise funds to finance his military enterprises. For another, American merchant ships became principal vehicles of trade for both France and Britain. And yet the warring European powers' efforts to cripple one another by hampering shipping increasingly put American shipping at risk.

Jefferson struggled to avoid taking sides with Napoleon or with the nations opposing him. Britain and France made his task harder, as their navies harassed American commercial ships. Each power issued orders and directives seeking to cripple its foe's oceangoing trade. The United States was caught between the two nations in a mesh of conflicting policies and commands, and American shipping repeatedly paid the price.

In 1806, Jefferson instructed James Monroe and William Pinkney of Maryland, the joint American ministers to Great Britain, to negotiate a treaty with Britain that would replace the much-hated Jay Treaty of 1795. In particular, he directed them to end the British practice of impressment and to reform other policies under which Britain had been inter-fering with American vessels trading with Britain and France. Impressment was the procedure by which British naval officers boarded other nations' ships and arrested and removed sailors whom British officers identified as deserters from the Royal Navy.

Americans hated impressment because it violated American sovereignty; in addition, many American sailors had deserted from British warships and feared being recap-tured. Unfortunately for Jefferson's hopes, Monroe and Pinkney could not secure the concessions that he had ordered them to win, and the President thought the Monroe-Pinkney Treaty no better than the Jay Treaty. Disgusted and disappointed, Jefferson refused to submit the treaty to the Senate. As he wrote to Madison on April 21, 1807, "I am more and more convinced that our best course is, to let the negotiation take a friendly nap, and endeavor in the meantime to practice on such of its principles as are mutually acceptable." One week after the signing of the Monroe-Pinkney Treaty, the British government announced new policies governing foreign trade that would have undermined the pact; this development persuaded Jefferson that he had made the right decision.

An incident in the summer of 1807 dramatized the problems facing the United States in an era of warring European powers. On June 22, 1807, the British frigate HMS *Leopard,* patrolling off the coast of Virginia, encountered the USS *Chesapeake.* Claiming that the American vessel harbored British deserters, the *Leopard* demanded that the *Chesapeake* produce its crew for inspection. When the *Chesapeake*'s captain refused, insisting that there were no deserters in his ranks, the *Leopard* fired four broadsides into the *Chesapeake,* killing three and wounding eighteen—including the captain—and forcing it to surrender for board-ing. The *Leopard* seized four sailors from the Chesapeake; only one proved to be a British deserter. The *Chesapeake-*

Leopard incident outraged the United States; as Jefferson observed, no incident since the battles of Lexington and Concord in 1775 had so unified the American people. Even New England Federalists, who usually supported Britain as the defender of civilization against atheist France, denounced the *Leopard*'s actions and demanded that Jefferson defend American rights.

The Jefferson administration insisted that the British government apologize and pay reparations for the loss of lives and the damage to the *Chesapeake,* but the British ignored the American claim. In response, on July 2, 1807, Jefferson issued a proclamation ordering all British ships to leave American waters; on July 5, he called for the raising of a 100,000-man militia to enforce his proclamation. Though popular sentiment might have welcomed an American declaration of war, Jefferson was wary of thrusting the United States into an all-out conflict with Britain. Instead, he decided to try a different kind of reprisal.

On December 22, 1807, Congress enacted the Embargo Act. This measure, Jefferson's and Madison's brainchild, barred American vessels from trading with or carrying goods for any European power. Jefferson and Madison had two aims: first, to keep American ships out of the paths of French or British vessels (thus avoiding repeats of the *Chesapeake-Leopard* affair), and, second, to use American commerce as an economic and diplomatic weapon. They hoped that cutting off the revenue from business with the U.S. would persuade Britain and France to make peace.

Unfortunately, Jefferson's and Madison's hopes were out of touch with the reality of the situation. The embargo had no effect on Napoleon's French Empire, which was virtually self-sufficient; Britain's trade and economy suffered slightly from the loss of American trade, but nowhere near enough to induce Britain to change its policies toward the Americans. Worse yet, the embargo was an economic disaster for the United States. Previously, spurred by the rapid growth of

In this mocking cartoon, Britain's King George III (left) and France's Emperor Napoleon I (right) steal money from President Jefferson's pockets. Jefferson tried to punish Britain and France by cutting off American trade, but his embargo only ruined the American economy.

business resulting from European wars, American foreign trade had reached levels of $108 million per year. During the 15 months of the embargo, it dropped by more than three-fourths, to $22 million per year. Further, the embargo hit New York and the New England states especially hard. Both merchants and sailors and their families suffered, as did those involved in the American economy's fledgling manufacturing sector.

The anger and suffering provoked by the embargo increasingly began to turn up in Jefferson's mail, bringing him some of the most anguished and enraged letters he ever received. One irate sailor in Philadelphia dared Jefferson to come and face him:

Dear Sir,

I wish you would take this embargo off as soon as you possibly can, for damn my eyes if I can live as it is. I shall certainly cut my throat, and if I do you will lose one of the best seaman that ever sailed. I have a wife and four young one's to support, and it goes damn'd hard with me now. If I dont cut my throat I will go join the English and fight against you. I hope, honored Sir, you will forgive the abrupt manner in which this is wrote as I am damn'd mad. But still if ever I catch you over there, take care of your honored neck.

Yours,

T. Selby

No. 9 Pine St. If you want to see him, you damn'd rascal.

In January 1808, Jefferson tried to tighten the embargo by applying it to inland waters and commerce over land. His target was the flourishing trade between the northern states and Canada, but his efforts were in vain. Spurred by economic hardship, merchants, ship captains, and traders took up smuggling. Vexed, Jefferson ordered the nation's armed forces to enforce the embargo, even within the United States; he sent units of the U.S. Army to patrol the frontiers and naval gunboats to major American harbors.

These measures violated cherished political principles, some of which Jefferson had given memorable expression. In the Declaration of Independence, he had denounced George III for using British military forces to enforce the law in the colonies in time of peace. Now, he was pursuing policies resembling those that he had cited in 1776 as grounds for independence and revolution. Jefferson even declared New York's Lake Champlain region, near the Canadian border, to be in a state of insurrection. Customs officers in such ports as Boston and New York were authorized to seize goods they suspected of violating the embargo, and U.S. naval vessels could stop, board, and search ships on the basis of mere suspicion. The President ignored the 4th Amendment's requirement of search warrants.

Vexed by the embargo's failure and by growing rebelliousness among New Englanders and New Yorkers, congressional leaders admitted that the embargo had failed. On March 1, 1809, three days before the end of Jefferson's term, Congress passed and Jefferson reluctantly signed into law the Non-Intercourse Act, which replaced the embargo with a milder set of economic sanctions targeting only Britain and France. This measure only postponed the seething problems that exploded as the War of 1812 during the Presidency of Jefferson's successor, James Madison—when, as a consequence of Jefferson's policies, the nation found itself unprepared for war.

On March 2, 1809, tired and embittered as his Presidency drew to a close, Jefferson wrote to Pierre S. du Pont de Nemours:

> Within a few days I retire to my family, my books and farms; and having gained the harbor myself, I shall look on my friends still buffeting the storm with anxiety indeed, but not with envy. Never did a prisoner released from his chains feel such relief as I shall on shaking off the shackles of power. Nature intended me for the tranquil pursuits of science, by rendering them my supreme delight. But the enormities of the times in which I have lived, have forced me to take a part in resisting them, and to commit myself on the boisterous ocean of political passion.

10

ENTHUSIASM AND ANGUISH (1809–1826)

On March 4, 1809, Thomas Jefferson stayed in Washington long enough to witness James Madison's inauguration. Then, in his definitive retreat from politics, he left for Virginia, seeking peace and restoration among his family, his friends, his books, and his lands. He never again left Virginia and showed no interest in doing so. For the last 17 years of his life, he assumed the role of an American sage.

Jefferson's favorite pastime in retirement was rebuilding Monticello. His beloved house was a country mansion, the headquarters of a large plantation, and a stage set designed to display the Sage of Monticello. Visitors to Monticello were ushered into the main foyer where, surrounded by relics from the Lewis and Clark expedition, maps, paintings, and portrait busts, they waited for Jefferson to enter and greet them. Legend has it that he would point out the two facing busts of himself and his great adversary Hamilton and comment, "Opposed in death as in life!" Visitors also noted that Monticello's eccentricities of design robbed the house of comfort for guests. The staircases were uncomfortably narrow and cramped, to ensure the greatest amount of open space on the main floor. Also, the house's exterior was

When the pressures of guests and rebuilding made Monticello too noisy and uncomfortable, Thomas Jefferson retreated to his second house, Poplar Forest, which he also designed himself.

designed to make it appear only one story tall; the windows of the second-floor guest rooms thus were only as high as guests' ankles or knees.

Monticello and its contents displayed Jefferson's habit of tinkering. He installed a new sundial on its grounds and built a "cannonball clock" into the main foyer; its cannonball weights, together with markings on the walls, tell not just the time of day but the day of the week. He also devised a set of doors between the hall and the parlor, both of which would open at a touch thanks to the operations of a hidden set of gears and chains. In his study, he installed his portable copying press, a device that he developed based on the traditional copying press used to make copies of letters and other documents and a copying machine or polygraph, which enabled a writer to make two copies of a page at the same time by means of linked pens.

One of the most famous objects at Monticello supposed to be a Jeffersonian invention is the revolving bookstand or music stand that allows five separate books or pieces of sheet music to be displayed at the same time. Though we do not know whether Jefferson devised it, we know that it was made at the carpentry shop (or "joinery") at Monticello during his lifetime. Two counterparts to the revolving bookstand are the revolving bookcase and a specially modified chair, based on the English Windsor revolving chair but with a writing arm and a leg rest added to Jefferson's specifications. Finally, in his bedroom, Jefferson had his bed constructed in an alcove between two rooms so that it could be hoisted upward when not in use, thus freeing the alcove for use as a doorway.

Jefferson continued to remodel his house until he no longer could afford to do so. For much of his retirement, he, his family, and many of his visitors were living in the middle of a construction site. When the press of visitors or the din of rebuilding became too much even for him to bear, he retreated to a second, more distant residence, Poplar Forest, which he began building in 1806 and first visited in 1809.

Jefferson claimed to have given up interest in current affairs, but he remained engaged with the issues and struggles of politics and diplomacy, advising Presidents James Madison and James Monroe on domestic and foreign policy. During the War of 1812, for example, he cheerfully predicted that the American conquest of Canada would be merely "a matter of marching"—only to discover, with the rest of the nation, that Canadians were determined to remain within the British Empire and that the United States was, for the most part, unable to achieve its military goals.

Nearly a decade later, in 1823, British Prime Minister George Canning proposed to the United States that the two nations jointly oppose Spanish attempts to reconquer Spain's former colonies in Latin America. Monroe referred the suggestion to Jefferson and Madison. Both men recommended accepting it in some form. Writing on October 24, 1823, Jefferson noted:

> Our first and fundamental maxim should be, never to entangle ourselves in the broils of Europe. Our second, never to suffer Europe to intermeddle with cis-Atlantic

*These architectural
drawings capture
Jefferson's labors to
create the University
of Virginia. Inspired by
the Pantheon in
Rome, the Rotunda
was the central build-
ing of the university.*

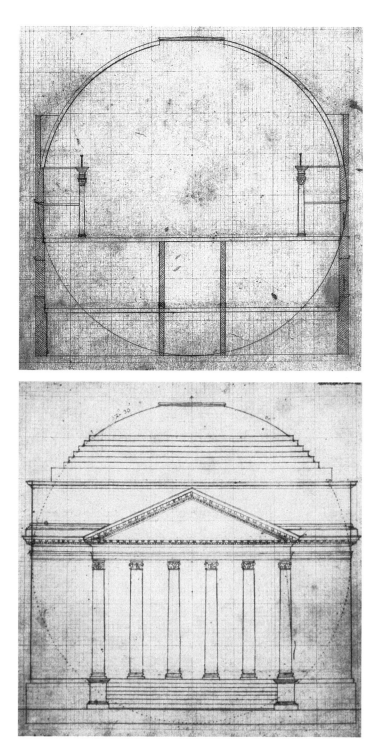

affairs. America, North and South, has a set of interests distinct from those of Europe, and peculiarly her own. She should therefore have a system of her own, separate and apart from that of Europe. While the last is laboring to become the domicil of despotism, our endeavor should surely be, to make our hemisphere that of freedom.

Jefferson reasoned that, "[b]y acceding to [Britain's] proposition, we detach [Britain] from the bands [of European tyrannies], bring her mighty weight into the scale of free government, and emancipate a continent at one stroke, which might otherwise linger long in doubt and difficulty." But Secretary of State John Quincy Adams, insisting that acting at Britain's suggestion would make the United States "a cockboat in the wake of a British man of war," persuaded Monroe to reject the British proposal and follow an independent course. In the annual message to Congress that he sent on December 2, 1823, Monroe warned that the United States would reject any attempt by European nations to interfere with the affairs of any nation in the Western Hemisphere. Later generations have called this principle the Monroe Doctrine.

Jefferson's last great public enterprise was his effort to found a new university in Virginia. He had first experimented with this idea in the late 1770s, when, as part of his campaign to revise Virginia's laws, he had proposed an educational system designed as a pyramid, with primary schools at the ward level, secondary schools at the county level, and a new university at the state level. For decades, he had hammered away at the cause of educational reform, despite the legislature's lack of interest.

The seed of Jefferson's new plans for a university was the Albemarle Academy, an institution of higher learning that was founded in 1803 but lacked teachers, students, and facilities. In 1814, Jefferson, elected a trustee of the academy, began to work to turn it first into an institution called Central College, and then into a university. In 1816, the Virginia legislature authorized the creation of Central

College, with Jefferson as rector, or presiding officer, and a Board of Visitors (including Monroe and Madison). Then, at Jefferson's urging, the legislature named a commission, which in 1818 convened at Rockfish Gap and elected him its chairman.

The "Rockfish Gap Report," which he drafted, sketched a university that in many ways was the lengthened shadow of one man. Most previous universities had been founded by religious groups (Harvard, Yale, William and Mary, the College of New Jersey) or had some tie to organized religion (Oxford and Cambridge), and had been designed to train members of the clergy. By contrast, this university would be governed by the principles of the Virginia Statute for Religious Freedom: religious liberty for all, separation of church and state, and the pivotal importance of secular learning. Jefferson's report stated the university's purposes, including:

> To form the statesmen, legislators, and judges on whom public prosperity and individual happiness are so much in demand;

> To expound the principles and structure of government, the laws which regulate the intercourse of nations, those formed municipally for our own government, and the sound spirit of legislation, which, banishing all arbitrary and unnecessary restraint on individual action, shall leave us free to do whatever does not violate the equal rights of another;

> To harmonize and promote the interests of agriculture, manufactures and commerce, and by well informed views of political economy to give a free scope to public industry;

> To develop the reasoning faculties of our youth, enlarge their minds, cultivate their morals, and install into them the precepts of virtue and order;

> To enlighten them with mathematical and physical sciences, which advance the arts, and administer to the health, subsistence, and comforts of human life;

And, generally, to form them to habits of reflection and correct action, rendering them examples of virtue to others, and happiness within themselves.

Having received its charter from the Virginia legislature in 1819, the new university took shape through the early 1820s. In nearly every feature, it was Jefferson's brainchild. Jefferson recruited its faculty and planned its curriculum. At the same time that he wanted to ensure that each student could craft his own educational program, he drew up lists of assigned course books and readings, taking special care in planning the teaching of politics, law, and natural philosophy. His goal was to strike a balance between freedom of inquiry and teaching (critics would call it indoctrinating) correct political principles.

Jefferson won the Rockfish Gap commission's approval for his preferred site for the university: the village of Charlottesville, conveniently close to Monticello. There he laid out its campus and designed its buildings, consulting the noted architect Benjamin Henry Latrobe and his bitter rival William Thornton (separately, so that each man did not know that Jefferson was in touch with the other). Drawing on the classical architectural models that he loved, he determined to realize his dream of an "academical village," which he had sketched in a letter in 1810:

It is infinitely better to erect a small and separate lodge for each separate professorship, with only a hall below for his class, and two chambers above for himself; joining these lodges by barracks for a certain portion of the students, opening into a covered way to give a dry communication between all the schools. The whole of these arranged around an open square of grass and trees, would make it, what it should be in fact, an academical village, instead of a large and common den of noise, of filth and of fetid air. It would afford that quiet retirement so friendly to study, and lessen the dangers of fire, infection, and tumult.

The university's centerpiece was its massive domed Rotunda, half the diameter of Rome's Pantheon, one of the greatest buildings of classical times. Branching from the two sides of the Rotunda were two long rows of buildings. These rows consisted of two-story "pavilions," each with a lecture room on the main floor and private apartments above for professors and their families; one-story "dormitories," each housing two students; "refectories," or dining halls; and "porticoes," or roofed walkways, along which students and professors could walk in any weather. Between the two rows lay a wide, grassy plain, the Lawn.

For nearly a decade, Jefferson labored unceasingly to bring his dream into reality. It was a difficult enterprise for anyone to undertake, and nearly miraculous considering that it dominated Jefferson's life when he was in his 70s and 80s. With grim determination, he confronted and overcame nearly every obstacle, resorting on occasion to political and personal arm-twisting. The establishment of the university was fraught with difficulties. It challenged Virginia's other institution of higher learning, the College of William and Mary; it seemed to some nervous conservatives to be a nursery of atheism and radicalism; and Jefferson's plan to recruit foreign scholars for the faculty offended some Virginians who believed that they had nothing to learn from the corrupt Old World.

The one battle that Jefferson lost was over Thomas Cooper, whom Jefferson wanted to become the university's professor of chemistry. The English-born Cooper had been a staunch supporter of Jefferson, so much so that he was convicted of sedition in 1800 and served six months in jail. Cooper and Jefferson had a mutual friend in the great chemist and theologian Rev. Joseph Priestley, famed as the discoverer of oxygen. Unfortunately for them, Priestley also was a founder of Unitarianism, a sect of Christianity that saw Jesus not as the son of God who performed miracles and was resurrected after his crucifixion, but rather as a great moral teacher and prophet. Jefferson agreed with Priestley's theological beliefs, but Virginia's Presbyterians

saw a dire threat to religion in any attempt to advance any friend of Priestley. They therefore launched a public campaign against Cooper. Ultimately Jefferson wrote an embarrassed letter to Cooper explaining the barriers to his appointment, and Cooper resigned his appointment, but pocketed a hefty fee representing a significant part of his expected salary.

On March 7, 1825, all this hard work seemed to have produced a triumph. On that day, the University of Virginia opened its doors, with its rector Jefferson welcoming the first students to enroll. Flanking the rector were Madison, Monroe, and other dignitaries. It was one of the happiest and proudest days of Jefferson's life.

Unfortunately, the students showed little inclination to behave like the serious scholars whom Jefferson had hoped to welcome. Instead, they carried on in ways resembling Jefferson's idle, boisterous classmates at William and Mary. Their favorite activities were drinking, gambling, and rioting, all of which Jefferson denounced as "vicious irregularities." In particular, the students' nighttime raids up and down the Lawn, known as "calathumps," alarmed and out-

Taken in 1868, this earliest known photograph of the University of Virginia shows the Rotunda, its flanking rows of buildings, and the famed Lawn as they looked when Jefferson served as the University's first rector.

raged him. Those who took part in calathumps wore masks to avoid being recognized and punished as they shouted and yelled, fired guns into the air and whirled noisemakers, broke windows, and otherwise made a ruckus.

Such carryings-on were common in university life in Britain and America, but special reasons fueled the boisterous calathumps at the University of Virginia. For one thing, the students resented what Jefferson thought was one of the University's greatest strengths—its handpicked faculty of European academics. For another, Jefferson's decision to house professors and students in close quarters backfired. Instead of exerting a moderating influence on the students, the professors found themselves on the firing line, exposed to the risk of violence at students' hands. Indeed, when some professors tried to quiet unruly students, the rioters assaulted them with bricks and canes.

Shocked and grieved, Jefferson asked the Board of Visitors to draw up a code of conduct for students. Then he called a meeting of the student body. Striding in, flanked by Madison and Monroe, Jefferson began to address the gathering, but his disappointment in their behavior overcame him, and he briefly gave way and wept. His tears did what his words might not have done, shaming the students into vowing better behavior. The Board of Visitors expelled the student rioters, and framed a rigorous code of conduct for the University.

Jefferson saw his educational mission in the broadest terms, launching an array of projects to educate the general public. For example, he labored to shape how future generations would understand the Revolution and those who led it. Because he had a keen understanding of the power of visual images to command the public imagination, he showered advice on artists such as John Trumbull—whom he had known since the 1780s, when Trumbull served as his secretary in Paris—about how to depict such great scenes as the presentation of the Declaration of Independence to Congress. He urged Trumbull to prepare a grand painting (which now hangs in the United States Capitol) and a range of engravings, some detailed and expensive for wealthier purchasers, others simpler and cheaper for the great body of the people. He also penned recollections of great men and collections of anecdotes to aid biographers and editors, and he encouraged the work of historians and archivists.

One step that Jefferson took to enlighten the American people was a response to a military disaster, and an unexpected way for him to bolster his own finances. The War of 1812 had gone badly for the United States. In the summer of 1814, a British army captured Washington, D.C., and burned the Capitol, including the congressional library and other public buildings, as revenge for the Americans' burning of York (Toronto). In response, Jefferson made an unprecedented proposal. On September 21, 1814, writing to Representative Samuel Harrison Smith of Maryland, Jefferson offered to sell his books to Congress. Noting that "there is in fact no subject to which a member of Congress may not have occasion to refer," he explained how he had amassed the largest, finest private library in the United States. He had intended to bequeath it to Congress at his death; now he agreed to accept whatever price Congress wished to pay, asking only that he be allowed to retain certain books of classical literature for his own pleasure until he died.

Federalist senators and representatives denounced the sale as a trick to enrich Jefferson at the people's expense. They had a point, though it was rather that Jefferson was especially hard-pressed and needed money to meet urgent debts. They also were wary of the books that the man they branded an infidel would try to foist on the American people—some in foreign languages, some dealing with subjects not directly relevant to Congress's business, and some perhaps attacking the cause of religion and morality. Nonetheless, Congress bought the library, paying Jefferson $23,950 for 6,487 books.

Jefferson devoted great care to arranging for the transportation of his library to the nation's capital. On May 8,

1815, he wrote to Smith with understandable pride, "[A]n interesting treasure is added to your city, now become the depository of unquestionably the choicest collection of books in the US, and I hope it will not be without some general effect on the literature of our country." Once he sold his library, Jefferson immediately began to build another one, confessing to John Adams, "I cannot live without books...." In 1851, a fire in the Capitol destroyed two-thirds of the library that the nation purchased from Jefferson. Even so, the Library of Congress, reborn thanks to Jefferson's aid, has grown into the world's largest and finest research library.

Those who opposed buying Jefferson's library for the nation might have taken further alarm from Jefferson's continuing fascination with the origins of Christianity and the teachings of Jesus. Fifteen years after his first attempt to codify "The Philosophy of Jesus," he returned to the task. Now he laid out, side by side, texts of the Four Gospels in Greek, Latin, English, and French. With a penknife, he cut out those extracts that, he believed, represented the authentic teachings of Jesus and the true events of his life. In the process, he dropped passages dealing with miracles, visitations of angels, and the resurrection of Jesus after his death. Arranging them chronologically, he pasted the extracts into a small pocketbook, which he kept by him for the rest of his life. It is not clear whether he intended this book for publication—to educate his countrymen to combat the forces of what he often called "priestcraft" and superstition—or solely for his own use, but *The Life and Morals of Jesus of Nazareth,* first published by Congress in 1904 after that body purchased the manuscript volume, has often been reprinted, sometimes misleadingly dubbed *The Jefferson Bible.*

In a vitally important component of his project of public education, Jefferson worked to organize his papers, to write his autobiography, and to record his version of the anguished politics of the early Republic. His autobiography, which he wrote in the first half of 1821, takes the story of his life from a sketch of his parents' ancestry to his return to America from France in late 1789. Although not as engaging as Benjamin Franklin's autobiography, it is a valuable memoir, especially for its accounts of debates in the 2nd Continental Congress.

For the recounting of the 1790s and his Presidency, Jefferson had a different plan. He was so outraged by Chief Justice John Marshall's authorized five-volume life of Washington, which he condemned as a Federalist tract, that he decided to present the "true" history of the early Republic. He wove together official documents—his opinions as secretary of state and his reports to Congress—with his notes of cabinet meetings and his scribbled memoranda of private conversations, anecdotes, rumors, and gossip. In Jefferson's view, this evidence was central to the practice of politics in the early Republic. Gossip and rumor were the touchstones of who was to be relied on and who was not, who was to be entrusted with power and who was not. Jefferson sought to preserve for posterity the true history lurking under the surface of official events. Later scholars took apart his three massive volumes of documents and published his memoranda of political gossip separately as the *Anas* (from a Latin word for "memoranda").

As Jefferson struggled to define the history he had helped to make, he was becoming a living symbol of that history, the Sage of Monticello. He used that role to great effect, but it often threatened to smother him. One of the dwindling number of leaders of the Revolution, he was an object of curiosity to hundreds of visitors. The most famous visitor was the Marquis de Lafayette, who in 1824 toured the nation whose independence he helped to win. On November 4, 1824, as a crowd of onlookers cheered, the 67-year-old Lafayette and the 81-year-old Jefferson tottered toward each other across Monticello's lawn and embraced, weeping, in a public display of friendship.

A month later, Senator Daniel Webster of Massachusetts wrote down his impressions of Jefferson:

Mr. Jefferson is . . . above six feet high, of an ample long frame, rather thin and spare. His head, which is not peculiar in its shape, is set rather forward on his shoulders, and his neck being long, there is, when he is walking or conversing, an habitual protrusion of it. It is still well covered with hair, which having once been red, and now turning gray, is of an indistinct sandy-color.

His eyes are small, very light, and now neither brilliant nor striking. His chin is rather long, but not pointed. His nose small, regular in its outline, and the nostrils a little elevated. His mouth is well formed and still filled with teeth: it is strongly compressed, bearing an expression of contentment and benevolence. . . . His limbs are uncommonly long, his hands and feet very large, and his wrists of an extraordinary size. His walk is not precise and military, but easy and swinging. He stoops a little, not so much from age as from natural formation. When sitting, he appears short, partly from the disproportionate length of his limbs. . . .

His general appearance indicates an extraordinary degree of health, vivacity, and spirit.

Webster also recorded Jefferson's doubts about Andrew Jackson's fitness for the Presidency. Declaring, "He is one of the most unfit men I know for such a place," Jefferson fretted that Jackson "has very little respect for laws or constitutions. . . ." Recalling his observations of Jackson during his time as vice president, Jefferson added, "His passions are terrible. When I was President of the Senate he was a Senator; and he could never speak on account of the rashness of his feelings. . . . I have seen him . . . often choke with rage."

Through the 1810s and 1820s, many visitors less distinguished than Lafayette and Webster—some not distinguished at all—descended on Monticello, armed with letters of introduction. As a Virginia gentleman, Jefferson felt bound to offer hospitality to all of them. Unfortunately, too many guests presumed on his goodwill, staying for days or weeks at a time, driving up his debts and draining his ability to keep his finances in order. One of his overseers, Edmund Bacon, bitterly recalled the burdens these visitors imposed on Jefferson:

> After Mr. Jefferson returned from Washington, he was for years crowded with visitors, and they almost ate him out of house and home. They were there all times of the year; but about the middle of June the travel would commence..., and then there was a perfect throng of visitors.... There was no tavern in all that country that had so much company.... He knew that it more than used up all his income from the plantation and every-thing else; but he was so kind and polite that he received all his visitors with a smile, and made them welcome.

Bacon suspected that many of Jefferson's visitors were less interested in meeting the great man than in finding free room and board.

Others besieged the former President through the mails, seeking his endorsement of books or projects, mining his memory, or pestering him for advice. With almost unfailing courtesy, he answered thousands of such letters, "drudging at the writing table" for hours every day, as he complained to John Adams on January 11, 1817. Now and then, when someone leaked his letters to newspapers, he found himself at the epicenter of an unwelcome controversy.

To Jefferson, letter writing was many things, pleasant and burdensome alike; perhaps most important, it was his primary means to pursue his scientific and religious inter-ests, by corresponding with friends and colleagues in America and Europe. The most significant of Jefferson's myriad correspondents was John Adams. Their exchanges of letters had begun in the late 1770s, soon after they befriended each other in the Continental Congress; they continued as fellow diplomats in the mid-1780s, but the partisan bitterness of the 1790s helped to rend their friend-ship, and the flow of letters ceased. It took the devoted labors of Benjamin Rush, the noted Philadelphia physician and a signer of the Declaration of Independence, to bring Adams and Jefferson back together.

For years, Rush urged each man to reach out to the other. Thin-skinned as ever, Jefferson insisted that he had done nothing to justify the breach and had suffered bitterly at the hands of Adams's supporters. By contrast, Adams, whose character blended crustiness and self-mocking humor, replied on Christmas Day 1811 that, although he saw no reason why he should write to Jefferson or Jefferson should write to him, "[t]ime and chance, however, or possibly design, may produce ere long a letter between us." A week later, on New Year's Day 1812, he kept his word; he sent Jefferson a gentle, friendly letter that spoke of a mysterious "parcel of homespun" that he had sent under separate cover. Jefferson embraced the chance to write to Adams, pouring out his friendship and his memories of the great days of the Revolution. A few days later, he received the parcel Adams had mentioned: a two-volume set of John Quincy Adams's 1810 *Lectures on Rhetoric and Oratory, Delivered to the Classes of Senior and Junior Sophisters in Harvard University*, which he welcomed with delight.

Thus resumed one of the great correspondences in the history of American letters. The two aged veterans genially sparred over issues of philosophy, history, language, religion, science, diplomacy, and politics. Adams could not resist

This copying machine was a godsend to Jefferson, who promoted it to friends and colleagues and tinkered with it to improve its operation. The machine used two linked pens, the second pen writing on a blank page anything that the user wrote with the first. Jefferson used it to keep copies of his extensive outgoing correspondence.

making an occasional barbed comment about politics or about his and Jefferson's contrasting views of such issues as the need for a navy, or about their mutual adversary Hamilton. Adams's letters are more open, spontaneous, and humorous, in keeping with his character. He delighted in referring to Jefferson, eight years his junior, as "Young Man." Jefferson wrote elegant, formal, philosophical letters—miniature essays, following the model of the correspondence of Cicero, whom he and Adams both revered.

On April 6, 1816, Jefferson told Adams, "I steer my bark with Hope in the head, leaving Fear astern." Rarely did he show this confidence more than in his private letter of July 12, 1816, to the Virginia reformer Samuel Kercheval. Jefferson unburdened himself on the defects of the Virginia constitution of 1776, against which he had spoken and written for 40 years. He recognized that one key barrier to constitutional reform was the reverence that his fellow citizens felt for the early leaders of the Revolution and their political handiwork:

> Some men look at constitutions with sanctimonious reverence, and deem them like the arc of the covenant, too sacred to be touched. They ascribe to the men of the preceding age a wisdom more than human, and suppose what they did to be beyond amendment. I knew that age well; I belonged to it, and labored with it. It deserved well of its country. It was very like the present, but without the experience of the present; and forty years of experience in government is worth a century of book-reading; and this they would say themselves, were they to rise from the dead.

Jefferson then expounded on the tasks of framing and replacing constitutions, in one of his most eloquent statements of faith in human beings' ability to govern themselves:

> I am certainly not an advocate for frequent and untried changes in laws and constitutions. I think moderate imperfections had better be borne with; because, when once known, we accommodate ourselves to them, and find practical means of correcting their ill effects. But I

know also, that laws and institutions must go hand in hand with the progress of the human mind. As that becomes more developed, more enlightened, as new discoveries are made, new truths disclosed, and manners and opinions change with the change of circumstances, institutions must advance also, and keep pace with the times. We might as well require a man to wear still the coat which fitted him when a boy, as civilized society to remain ever under the regimen of their barbarous ancestors.

Despite his bold expressions of faith in the future, in the 1810s and 1820s he disagreed more and more with the development of the United States, as economic forces and technological change helped to knit the states together as a nation. In particular, he watched with agony as issues linked to slavery and its expansion became ever more central to American politics. He was torn by the conflict between his early antislavery convictions and his equally firm belief that slavery was an insoluble problem for the South in general and for Virginians in particular.

To the extent that he still believed that something could be done about slavery, he always linked abolition with exile of the freed slaves. His conviction grew that blacks and whites could not live together, side by side, in the same country in peace, and he became increasingly certain that freed slaves should be sent westward, or to Haiti in the Caribbean, or to Africa. As he aged, Jefferson became more Virginian in his constitutional and political outlook; he saw the series of controversies over slavery as a growing series of threats to the interests of his native state and region and to his conception of the Union, and he plunged further into despair on the issue.

Few episodes more strongly evoked his fears than the controversy over the admission of Missouri to the Union. On April 22, 1820, he explained his feelings to John Holmes. As a U.S. representative from the Maine district of Massachusetts, Holmes had backed Missouri's bid for statehood, defying his constituents' opposition to the admission of another slave state to the Union. Having acted in the hope that statehood for Missouri might also bring statehood for Maine in its wake, Holmes resigned his seat and sent Jefferson a copy of his letter to his constituents explaining his reasons for resigning.

In his letter thanking Holmes, Jefferson declared the Missouri question "this momentous controversy, [which] like a fire bell in the night, awakened and filled me with terror. I considered it at once as the knell of the Union." Jefferson further explained what he saw as the insoluble problems posed by the existence of slavery: "[W]e have the wolf by the ears. We can neither hold him, nor safely let him go. Justice is in one scale, and self-preservation in the other." In Jefferson's view, the famous Missouri Compromise that seemed to end the crisis was "a reprieve only, not a final sentence." He concluded bitterly:

> I regret that I am now to die in the belief, that the useless sacrifice of themselves by the generation of 1776, to acquire self-government and happiness to their country, is to be thrown away by the unwise and unworthy passions of their sons, and that my only consoliation is to be, that I live not to weep over it. If they would but dispassionately weigh the blessings they will throw away, against an abstract principle more likely to be effected by union than by scission, they would pause before they would perpetrate this act of suicide on themselves, and of treason against the hopes of the world.

The focus of Jefferson's fears was the attempt by Northern and Western representatives and senators to use national constitutional power to limit the spread of slavery. In Jefferson's eyes, that step would wreak havoc on the Constitution, which, he insisted, granted no power to the general government to limit slavery's spread. It was not his loyalty to slavery that stirred his anguish; rather, it was the threat to his vision of the federal Union that filled him with dread. Jefferson did not see his devotion to American nationalism as clashing with his commitment to state sovereignty; rather, he saw the two as complementing each other. He rejected what he saw as the North's nationalism of coercion from above. His version of American nationhood had at its core a Union of sovereign states, held together by shared ties of affection and interest, each of which would regulate its own affairs, including the decisions whether to accept or reject slavery on joining the Union, or to preserve or abolish slavery thereafter.

The most direct and pressing threat to Jefferson's peace of mind, however, was his growing burden of debt, much of it having roots dating back more than half a century. His calculations of the revenue he could earn from farming were always hopelessly optimistic; the windfall he had earned from selling his library to the United States already had been swallowed up by growing demands on his purse, and his need to keep up his position as a leader of Virginia's planter elite and as a hospitable host to scores of visitors plunged him ever deeper into debt. Two blows six years apart toppled his financial house of cards. In March of 1819, he agreed to cosign a note for a close friend and political ally, Wilson Cary Nicholas. Cosigning the note meant that Jefferson was promising Nicholas's creditor that if Nicholas could not repay the loan, the creditor could go to Jefferson for the money.

Backing a friend's loan was a common practice; no gentleman would insult a friend by refusing such a favor, so Jefferson agreed to put himself at risk. In August of 1819, however, Martha Jefferson Randolph urgently wrote to her father that Nicholas's financial empire was crashing to ruin. Soon afterward Nicholas confessed with "mortification" that he could not pay the note that Jefferson had endorsed. Nicholas's default put Jefferson on the spot. Not only did he have to shoulder a huge, unexpected debt, but he also had to pay $1,200 a year in interest, and this burden continued for years after Nicholas died, bankrupt and humiliated, in 1820. Then, in 1825, agricultural prices, the value of the lands pledged as security for debts, and the value of paper money all plunged simultaneously—but the demands of Jefferson's creditors remained constant. Jefferson's finances, already weakened by the Nicholas debacle, were shattered.

For decades, Jefferson had comforted himself with wildly optimistic predictions and estimates about the rate of return on his farms and his finances, but now he could not deny the truth any longer: he faced the loss of all he had. Sadly, he petitioned the state legislature to permit him to sell most of his lands by a lottery, which would raise enough money for him to meet his obligations and perhaps retain Monticello and one farm.

Martha Jefferson Randolph, the only one of the six children of Thomas Jefferson and Martha Wayles Jefferson to survive both her parents, fiercely defended her father's reputation in later years.

Although at first the legislature refused, it reconsidered, sponsoring a lottery to raise money for him. Meanwhile, his friends raised funds to ease his financial woes. Even with their help, Jefferson's near-bankruptcy made it impossible for him to free his slaves—though there is no evidence that he planned to do so. All he could do was to free the children of Sally Hemings, thus keeping the promise he had made to her long before, as reported by her son Madison Hemings. (Martha Jefferson Randolph turned a blind eye when Sally Hemings herself left Monticello to live with her children in the free state of Ohio.) Jefferson's hope that Martha and her husband, Thomas Mann Randolph, would inherit Monticello and be able to hold it for the rest of their lives was doomed.

Thus, at his life's close, Jefferson wrestled with fears and anxieties public and private, national and personal. Other members of the Revolutionary generation shared his doubts. In 1802, Alexander Hamilton had noted sadly in a private letter, "Every day proves to me more and more that this American world was not made for me." So, too, such leading figures as George Washington and John Jay all had come close to despair in pondering the future of the American experiment. In particular, Jefferson was a victim of the painful paradox that beset nearly all Virginia's gentleman farmers. The social and economic forces unleashed by the Revolution that they had helped to create had undermined the genteel, ordered world into which they had been born, and made life as they knew it and wanted to live it all but impossible.

Jefferson had to suffer other indignities as well. For most of his retirement, he had enjoyed good health, and visitors often remarked on his vigor. In early 1826, however, his physical condition began to decline. At 80, he still rode a horse and stood ramrod-straight, but now he was feeling the weight of his years; as he approached 83, various ailments, including diabetes, arthritis, a urinary tract infection, and (some biographers suggest) colon cancer, combined to sap his strength. His failing finances and his fears for his beloved Virginia added to his burdens. These worries increasingly broke through the polished surface of his letters.

On July 3, Jefferson fell sick with a fever. Through the night, he asked, "Is it the Fourth?" Just before midnight, his grandson, Thomas Jefferson Randolph, and his doctor, Robley Dunglison, told him, "It soon will be." He smiled and sank back on his sickbed. After asking that his pillows be adjusted so that he could lie more comfortably, he fell into a coma.

On July 4, 1826, the fiftieth anniversary of the adoption of the Declaration of Independence, at ten minutes before one o'clock in the afternoon, Thomas Jefferson died, nearly three months after his eighty-third birthday. Five hours later, John Adams, eight months past his ninetieth birthday, sat propped in his favorite chair in his study at the Adams house in Quincy, Massachusetts. Breathing with difficulty, Adams spoke: "Thomas Jefferson..." His voice trailed off, and none standing by could catch his closing words as he died. The

"ALL EYES ARE OPENED, OR OPENING, TO THE RIGHTS OF MAN"

Writing on June 24, 1826, in what would be his last letter from his pen, Thomas Jefferson apologized to Washington, D.C., mayor Roger C. Weightman that his health prevented him from attending the celebration of the 50th anniversary of the Declaration of Independence in the nation's capital. This letter was Jefferson's "farewell address," restating his faith in the American Revolution and in the future of democracy.

May it be to the world, what I believe it will be, (to some parts sooner, to others later, but finally to all,) the signal of arousing men to burst the chains under which monkish ignorance and superstition had persuaded them to bind themselves, and to assume the blessings and security of self-government. That form which we have substituted, restores the free right to the unbounded exercise of reason and freedom of opinion. All eyes are opened, or opening, to the rights of man. The general spread of the light of science has already laid open to every view the palpable truth, that the mass of mankind has not been born with saddles on their backs, nor a favored few booted and spurred, ready to ride them legitimately, by the grace of God. These are grounds of hope for others. For ourselves, let the annual return of this day forever refresh our recollections of these rights, and an undiminished devotion to them. I should, indeed, with peculiar delight, have met and exchanged there, congratulations personally with the small band, the remnant of that host of worthies, who joined with us, on that day, in the bold and doubtful election we were to make, for our country, between submission, or the sword; and to have enjoyed with them the consolatory fact that our fellow citizens, after half a century of experience and prosperity, continue to approve the choice we made.

Adams family later reported his dying words as "Thomas Jefferson survives. . . ."

When the nation learned that two of its greatest men had died on the same day, and on such a notable anniversary, many Americans saw in the event the hand of God. They wondered whether succeeding generations could preserve the fruits of the Revolution that Adams, Jefferson, and their allies had helped to lead.

At the end, Thomas Jefferson was caught between past and future, between his origins and his aspirations for himself and the nation, between who he was and what he wanted to be. The reasons for his ruin lay in part in what he hoped posterity would deem his most enduring legacy—the American Revolution. The new democratic world that he envisioned had dwindling room for the dignified, elegant, free-spending gentlemen farmers who, he hoped, would govern that world. Rather, the forces he helped to set in motion ground him and his hopes for his family's fortunes to pieces. Even so, he succeeded beyond his hopes, for his identification with the Revolution and with what posterity saw as its core principles—principles that he voiced with surpassing eloquence—defines his image to this day.

Other things shaping that image are the unresolved contradictions in his thinking, and his occasional evasiveness and hypocrisy. Jefferson could not resolve the conflicts his soaring words helped to define—conflicts that plagued his life, polarized his thought, envenomed his politics, and terrorized his last years—conflicts from which, increasingly, he averted his eyes. The clash between his professed ideals and his life's realities is as bitter as the clash that it exemplifies, between the nation's creed—which he did so much to shape—and its history.

EPILOGUE:
"TAKE CARE OF ME
WHEN DEAD. . . . "

In February 1826, ailing and debt-ridden, Thomas Jefferson wrote to James Madison: "To myself you have been a pillar of support through life. Take care of me when dead, and be assured that I shall leave with you my last affections." Succeeding generations of Americans have found various ways to take care of Jefferson and to understand his complex, ambiguous legacies. The story of "what history has made of Thomas Jefferson," a phrase coined by the historian Merrill D. Peterson, falls into four stages.

From Jefferson's death in 1826 until the end of the Civil War in 1865, the controversy that swirled around him in life continued. In an age of devotion to organized religion, Americans hailed Jefferson as a champion of religious freedom—or damned him as a godless enemy to true faith. So, too, in an era increasingly torn by sectional antagonism over slavery and its expansion, Americans in the North and West praised Jefferson as a staunch defender of liberty and equality—or denounced him as a dangerous advocate of slavery and inequality—while Americans in the South praised him as an advocate of state sovereignty—or denounced him as a fuzzy-minded idealist for his writings on the evils of slavery. Finally, when issues clustered around slavery posed urgent challenges to the Union, Jefferson was seen as the spokesman of American nationalism—or the father of state sovereignty, nullification, and secession.

From the 1860s through the 1920s, Jefferson's historical reputation sank to its lowest ebb, an indirect casualty of the Civil War. Abraham Lincoln had claimed Jefferson as his intellectual hero and declared that, as President, he would be guided by Jeffersonian principles. Indeed, his 1863 Gettysburg Address made the Declaration of Independence, not the Constitution, the founding charter of the United States. In the decades following Lee's surrender to Grant at Appomattox Courthouse, however, many historians denounced Jefferson as the inventor of secession, charging that his ideas had inspired John C. Calhoun, Jefferson Davis, and the Confederacy.

An urban and industrial America found dwindling relevance in the prophecies of the man who dreamed of a rural republic of yeoman farmers, and whose papers teemed with attacks on cities, manufacturing, and centralized government power. For them, Hamilton, not Jefferson, captured the essence of America. Also, as more of Jefferson's papers became available, scholars found growing evidence of what they called his dishonesty. In the early 20th century, Progressive historians praised Jefferson's critiques of moneyed wealth and the corrupting alliance of business and government, and his championing of "the many" against "the few." Even so, they still disdained him as, in the words of President Woodrow Wilson, "not a great American."

The third era of Jefferson's reputation had its roots in the popular revulsion against the excesses of the "Roaring Twenties." The 1929 stock market crash and the Great Depression sent the historical seesaw tilting back Jefferson's way. President Franklin Delano Roosevelt embraced Jefferson, hailing his predecessor's combat against "malefactors of great wealth," his championing of the rights of the common man, and his criticism of an unelected Supreme Court's use of judicial review. Some mocked Roosevelt's attempts to cast himself as Jefferson's heir, arguing that the "big government" associated with the New Deal would have horrified Jefferson. Roosevelt and his supporters answered that they were using Hamiltonian means (activist, vigorous national government) to achieve Jeffersonian ends (liberty and justice for the great body of the people and restraint of the power of concentrated wealth).

The coming of the Second World War in 1939 and American entry into that war in 1941 spurred Jefferson's return to heroic stature. Roosevelt declared that Americans were fighting Nazi and Fascist tyranny to defend the cause of Jeffersonian democracy. That the nation marked the bicentennial of Jefferson's birth in 1943, during one of the darkest times of the Second World War, further enshrined Jefferson as the heroic advocate of liberty and democracy. In the 1940s, with the beginnings of the "cold war" against the USSR, the United States was desperate for an ideology to pit against Communism. Thus, American leaders and educators embraced Jeffersonian democracy as re-imagined by scholars of the 1930s. Growing battles over religious liberty and separation of church and state from the 1940s to the 1960s confirmed Jefferson as the defining symbol of American values.

In this era, Americans created five monuments to Jefferson. First, in 1938 the U.S. Mint replaced the Indian Head nickel with a design showing Jefferson in profile, based on Houdon's famous bust, with Monticello on the reverse. Second, 1941 witnessed the completion of Gutzon Borglum's titanic sculpture on Mount Rushmore in South Dakota's Black Hills, featuring Jefferson along with Washington, Lincoln, and Theodore Roosevelt. Third, on April 13, 1943 (Jefferson's 200th birthday), President Roosevelt dedicated the Jefferson Memorial in Washington, D.C. Its design echoed the dome of Monticello and the Palladian architecture that Jefferson admired; the Jefferson quotations on its walls portray him as the champion of democracy for the modern world. Fourth, in 1948 the noted historian Dumas Malone published the first of a six-volume, encyclopedic, learned, and sympathetic biography, which he completed in 1981. Fifth, in 1950 President Harry S. Truman ordered that the federal government fund a national program to put the primary sources of the history of American democracy within the reach of every American who had access to a research library. The enterprise's centerpiece was the comprehensive edition of *The Papers of Thomas Jefferson* based at Princeton University. Founded by Julian Boyd, the Jefferson Papers project continues to this day and promises to fill 75 to 100 volumes.

In the 1960s, a fourth, more critical stage in the history of Jefferson's reputation began to emerge, spurred, ironically, by the fruits of the documentary editing revolution launched by *The Papers of Thomas Jefferson*. Now that so much evidence of Jefferson's life was becoming readily available, scholars could pose troubling questions shaped by the concerns of a new era. The struggle for racial equality unleashed a host of inquiries into Jefferson's views of blacks and slavery. Scholars pursuing these topics cast bleak light on Jefferson's record as a slaveholder, a racial theorist, and a faltering opponent of slavery. New study of Native American history raised its own set of doubts about Jefferson, so long hailed as a champion of the rights of Indian nations. The rise of women's history exposed Jefferson's less than enlightened view of women's abilities and his blunt reluctance to extend his democratic ideology to embrace women. Finally, and most dramatically, there is the case of Sally Hemings.

At first, many Americans brushed aside the Hemings charges first made public in 1802 by James Thomson Callender as the vicious lies of a drunken dealer in rumor and slander. Jefferson's daughter, Martha Jefferson Randolph; his grandson, Thomas Jefferson Randolph; his granddaughter, Ellen Jefferson Coolidge; and his authorized biographer, Henry S. Randall, all denied them. Abolitionists cited the

Monticello today strikes visitors as elegant and peaceful, enshrining Jefferson's values and commemorating his life. In his lifetime, however, it was more a construction site than a finished residence, as he regularly experimented with its layout and design.

charges repeatedly in the years before the Civil War, however, and they inspired the first major African-American novel, William Wells Brown's *Clotel, or the President's Daughter.* In 1873, in an interview with an Ohio newspaper, the *Pike County Republican,* Madison Hemings, a retired master carpenter then in his sixties, insisted that he and his brothers and sisters were Jefferson's children. In this interview, Hemings gave a detailed account of his mother's life and his own observations of Jefferson—an account backed up by another ex-slave, Israel Jefferson, who was interviewed by the same newspaperman. Scholars ignored these autobiographical accounts for nearly a century.

In 1968, Winthrop D. Jordan's *White over Black,* a pathbreaking examination of white Americans' ideas about blacks, was the first major historical study to take the

Hemings story seriously. In 1974, Fawn Brodie's *Thomas Jefferson: An Intimate History* made the most sustained argument to date that Jefferson had a sexual relationship with Hemings. Critics mocked her book's sweeping use of Sigmund Freud's psychological theories and her occasional historical errors. Also in that year, a collection of essays by a revered figure in American scholarship seemed to refute the Hemings story. *Fame and the Founding Fathers: Essays of Douglass Adair* included Adair's unfinished essay, "The Jefferson Scandals," naming Jefferson's nephews Peter and Samuel Carr as the fathers of Sally's children. Adair's reputation for historical detective work, plus his fame as a leading scholar of the Revolutionary generation, stamped his essay as the last word on the controversy.

A curious disconnect followed, with most Jefferson specialists rejecting the idea of a Hemings-Jefferson liaison and most historians of the Revolutionary, Confederation, and early national periods accepting it. There matters rested until 1997, when Professor Annette Gordon-Reed of New York Law School, a specialist in the law of evidence, revisited the issue. Her *Thomas Jefferson and Sally Hemings: An American Controversy* presented a thorough analysis of the evidence and the ways that scholars had treated it. First, she showed that generations of Jefferson scholars had dismissed the Hemings claims because of their unexamined assumptions about historical evidence and credibility, such as "slaves lie," "black people lie," and "white people tell the truth." Second, cross-checking the Hemings's oral traditions supporting the relationship with documentary evidence not available to them, she demonstrated that these two bodies of historical evidence confirmed each other. She thus convinced many readers and historians that Sally Hemings had a sexual relationship with Thomas Jefferson and had children with him.

Soon after the appearance of Gordon-Reed's study, a team of geneticists launched a research project using the new technique of DNA analysis. They secured DNA samples from people in direct male line of descent from five men: Thomas Jefferson's uncle, Field Jefferson; Eston Hemings, Sally Hemings's youngest son; Peter and Samuel Carr; and Thomas Woodson, another of Jefferson's slaves who, his descendants insist, was the first son of Thomas Jefferson and Sally Hemings. In November 1998, the geneticists published an article in the distinguished British science journal *Nature* explaining the results of their tests. They concluded that Eston Hemings was the child of a male member of Jefferson's family; that neither Peter nor Samuel Carr could have fathered Eston Hemings; and that Thomas Woodson was not descended from Thomas Jefferson. Putting together the historical evidence and the DNA results, the authors of the *Nature* study concluded that the person most likely to have fathered Eston Hemings was Thomas Jefferson himself.

Finally, in January 2000, a statistician on the staff of the Thomas Jefferson Memorial Foundation analyzed the odds that anyone other than Jefferson was the father of Eston Hemings. He used the pattern first noticed by Winthrop Jordan of Jefferson's presence on the scene nine months before each time that Sally Hemings gave birth and the lack of proof of any other person's presence as a potential father all those times. He concluded that the odds against anyone but Jefferson being the father were ten thousand to one.

Rarely in the writing of American history has the conventional wisdom about a debate reversed course so completely. The new consensus that the Jefferson–Hemings relationship did exist rests on three pillars: the close analysis of circumstantial evidence and oral tradition in Annette Gordon-Reed's book, the DNA study published in *Nature,* and the statistical analysis. Recent attempts by "Jefferson defenders" to substitute Jefferson's brother Randolph as the father, or to suggest that Sally Hemings had sexual relationships with more than one man (none of them being Jefferson), are notable for the heat with which their supporters argue them, but not for the light that they shed on this controversy.

These developments raised further troubling questions about Jefferson's character. It was bad enough that Jefferson owned slaves. Worse still, he had presented in *Notes on the State of Virginia* a racist case against sexual relations between blacks and whites and an equally disturbing argument that freed slaves should be deported to Africa or the Caribbean. What then are we to make of Jefferson's sexual relationship with one of his slaves? Was it rape—a slaveholder's exercise of his "right" to use a female slave as he saw fit, with her having no say in the matter? Was Jefferson's bitter attack on interracial sex an expression of racism, an act of profound hypocrisy, or both? Could the relationship between Jefferson and Sally Hemings have been loving, as well as sexual, rather than rape? How did Jefferson's two families at Monticello—one white (his daughter Martha, her husband, and their children) and one black (the Hemingses)—coexist? It is difficult, if not impossible, to answer these questions, because there is so little evidence.

What are we to make of Thomas Jefferson, 200 years after his inauguration as President, and nearly two centuries after his death? In 1874, the biographer James Parton wrote, "If Jefferson was wrong, America is wrong. If America is right, Jefferson was right." Parton grounded his observation on Jefferson's writing of the Declaration of Independence, the core document of the American political tradition and a classic statement of democratic values that continues to influence those seeking democracy and self-government around the world.

Not just the Declaration, however, explains Jefferson's influence. As Abraham Lincoln, the only American rivaling Jefferson in Americans' hearts, argued, Jefferson's principles are "the definitions and axioms of free society." When we seek to understand liberty, equality, progress, constitutional governance, separation of church and state, and the meaning of the American Revolution, we do so in contexts framed by Jefferson's writings and arguments. Whatever we think of

Jefferson as a person or as a politician, we can never take away from him his remarkable gift as a writer or his ultimate claims to fame. He achieved his intention to express "the American mind" and became the leading spokesman for the revolution of ideas that changed, and that continues to change, the face of America and the world. His words mean not only what he might have intended them to mean, but also what succeeding generations of Americans have read into them. Thus, whether he would even comprehend the United States in the first years of the 21st century, Jefferson's shadow looms large over us, thanks to the conflicting influences of his thinking, his doing, and—most important—his writing. That truth alone requires each generation to reacquaint itself with the life and work of Thomas Jefferson, and to grapple with his ambiguous legacies.

Thomas Jefferson joined George Washington, Abraham Lincoln, and Theodore Roosevelt in the titanic sculpture on the face of Mount Rushmore in South Dakota's Black Hills.

CHRONOLOGY

1743
April 13 [April 2, O.S.], Thomas Jefferson born in Shadwell, Virginia

1760
Begins studies at William and Mary (graduates 1762)

1767
Admitted to Virginia bar after studying law with George Wythe (1762–67)

1768
Elected to Virginia House of Burgesses

1769
Begins building first version of Monticello

1772
January 1, marries Martha Wayles Skelton (b. 1748)

1774
Writes "A Summary View of the Rights of British America" (published 1775)

1775
Chosen as delegate to Second Continental Congress

1776
Drafts Declaration of Independence

1777
Launches effort to revise laws of Virginia

1779
Elected governor of Virginia

1781
British troops force Virginia state government to flee, briefly capture Monticello; retires from public life

1782
Martha Jefferson dies

1783
Returns to public life as Virginia delegate to Confederation Congress

1784
Journeys to France on diplomatic mission

1785
Succeeds Franklin as American minister to France

1786
Enactment of Virginia Statute for Religious Freedom

1787
Publishes first public edition of *Notes on the State of Virginia*

1788
Possible beginning of relationship with Sally Hemings (b. 1773)

1789
Leaves France for United States

1790
Accepts appointment as secretary of state

1791
Growing rift with Treasury Secretary Alexander Hamilton

1793
Retires as secretary of state

1795
Begins elaborate rebuilding of Monticello

1796
Republican candidate for President; elected Vice President under John Adams

1798
Drafts Kentucky Resolutions calling for nullification of Alien and Sedition Acts

1800
Republican candidate for President; defeats John Adams, but ties with Aaron Burr

1801
House declares Jefferson elected as third President after 36 ballots; delivers his first inaugural address

1802
Begins to plan for possibility of acquiring New Orleans from French

1803
Lays groundwork for Lewis and Clark Expedition; Louisiana Purchase negotiated

1804
Lewis and Clark Expedition begins (ends 1806); re-elected as President

1806
Issues first proclamation against Burr conspiracy

1807
Burr arrested, tried, and acquitted of treason; embargo legislation enacted

1809
Embargo repealed; retires from public life and returns to Monticello

1812
Resumes correspondence with John Adams

1815
Congress purchases Jefferson's library to rebuild Library of Congress

1818
Writes Rockfish Gap Commission Report proposing University of Virginia

1821
Writes Autobiography

1825
Rector of the University of Virginia

1826
Writes last letter; dies at Monticello on July 4

FURTHER READING
AND WEBSITES

BOOKS BY JEFFERSON

Jefferson, Thomas. *Notes on the State of Virginia,* ed. William Peden. Chapel Hill: University of North Carolina Press, 1955.

Koch, Adrienne, and William Peden, eds. *The Life and Selected Writings of Thomas Jefferson.* New York: Modern Library, 1943.

Onuf, Peter, ed. *Thomas Jefferson: An Anthology.* St. James, N.Y.: Brandywine, 1999.

Padover, Saul K., ed. *The Complete Jefferson.* New York: Duell, Sloan, and Pearce, 1943.

Peterson, Merrill D., ed. *The Portable Thomas Jefferson.* New York: Viking Penguin, 1976.

————. *Thomas Jefferson: Writings.* New York: Library of America, 1984.

BOOKS ABOUT JEFFERSON AND HIS TIME

Becker, Carl L. *The Declaration of Independence: A Study in the History of Political Ideas.* Rev. ed., New York: Knopf, 1945.

Bullock, Steven C. *The American Revolution: A History in Documents.* New York: Oxford University Press, 2003.

Cunningham, Noble E., Jr. *In Pursuit of Reason: The Life of Thomas Jefferson.* Baton Rouge: Louisiana State University Press, 1987.

Freeman, Joanne B. *Affairs of Honor: National Politics in the New Republic.* New Haven: Yale University Press, 2001.

Gordon-Reed, Annette. *Thomas Jefferson and Sally Hemings: An American Controversy.* Expanded ed., Charlottesville: University Press of Virginia, 1999.

Irving, Benjamin H. *Samuel Adams: Son of Liberty, Father of Revolution.* New York: Oxford University Press, 2002.

Maier, Pauline. *American Scripture: Making the Declaration of Independence.* New York: Knopf, 1997.

Miller, John C. *The Federalist Era, 1789–1800.* New York: Harper, 1960.

————. *The Wolf by the Ears: Thomas Jefferson and Slavery.* New York: Free Press, 1977.

Nash, Gary B. *Landmarks of the American Revolution*. New York: Oxford University Press, 2003.

Peterson, Merrill D. *Adams and Jefferson: A Revolutionary Dialogue*. Athens: University of Georgia Press, 1976.

———. *Thomas Jefferson and the New Nation*. New York: Oxford University Press, 1970.

Ellis, Joseph J., ed., *Thomas Jefferson: Genius of Liberty*. New York: Viking Studio, 2000.

WEBSITES

The Thomas Jefferson Papers

http://memory.loc.gov/ammem/mtjhtml/mtjhome.html

The website of the Library of Congress/American Memory project, which presents the Library of Congress collection of Jefferson's papers in searchable form.

Library of Congress Thomas Jefferson Exhibition

www.loc.gov/exhibits/jefferson

The online version of a Library of Congress exhibition marking the 200th anniversary of Jefferson's election as President in 1800.

Thomas Jefferson Digital Archive

http://etext.lib.virginia.edu/jefferson

Includes the searchable online version of John P. Foley's *Jeffersonian Cyclopedia* (New York: Funk & Wagnalls, 1900), Frank Shuffleton's bibliography of writings about Jefferson from 1826 through 1997, and a searchable collection of Jefferson letters.

Historic Sites

Colonial Williamsburg

Williamsburg, VA 23187
757-229-1000
www.history.org

Midway between Richmond and Norfolk, Williamsburg was the capital of Virginia from the late 1690s through 1780, when Governor Jefferson signed the legislation moving the capital to Richmond. The heart of the city is now a historical museum where visitors can experience the Williamsburg where the young Jefferson attended college and studied and practiced law, where he served as a member of the Virginia House of Burgesses, a revisor of Virginia's laws, and as governor of the state in 1779–1780.

Independence National Historical Park

Sixth and Market Street
Philadelphia, PA 19106
215-597-8974
www.nps.gov/inde/

Located in the heart of Philadelphia, Independence National Historical Park has at its core the old Pennsylvania State House (which we know as Independence Hall), where the Second Continental Congress met and adopted the Declaration of Independence; Congress Hall, where Vice President Jefferson presided over the Senate from 1797 through 1800; and the American Philosophical Society, of which Jefferson was the third president. Other buildings in the area include the boardinghouse where Jefferson lived when he drafted the Declaration of Independence.

Monticello

931 Thomas Jefferson Parkway
Charlottesville, VA 22902
434-984-9800
www.monticello.org

Monticello is the home that Thomas Jefferson built for himself and his family, and it also was home to a community of about 100 people, both free and enslaved, who worked there. Jefferson and other members of his family are buried in the cemetery on the grounds.

Poplar Forest

1008 Poplar Forest Drive
Forest, VA 24551
434–525–1806
www.poplarforest.org

Poplar Forest, a house that Jefferson built for himself in the early 19th century and used as a refuge from Monticello, is now a National Historic Landmark. Visitors to the site can take a 40-minute guided tour, which explores (among other topics) Jefferson's design and construction of his retreat, his landscape design, the plantation community, and the rescue and restoration of the property.

The University of Virginia

The Rotunda
Charlottesville, VA 22904
434–924–3239
www.virginia.edu

The University of Virginia, the greatest project undertaken by Thomas Jefferson during his retirement, is one of his architectural masterpieces. Visitors can take free guided tours of the Rotunda and the Lawn, and the University provides brochures outlining walking tours of the "Academical Village," the Rotunda, and the Pavilion Gardens.

INDEX

Illustrations and their captions are indicated by page numbers in **bold.**

ACKNOWLEDGMENTS

Nancy Toff suggested writing this book. Throughout its planning and writing, my admiration has grown for her energy, her shrewd and expert editing, and her mastery of the ins and outs of publishing. I am also grateful to her colleagues at Oxford University Press: Janielle S. Keith, Karen Fein, and Brigit Dermott. In particular, I am grateful to Nancy Hirsch for her patience and encouragement during the copyediting process, and to Jane Coughran for her invaluable aid in securing the book's illustrations.

Thanks to my family—my mother, Marilyn Bernstein, my sister, Linda A. Bernstein, and my brother, Steven J. Bernstein—who cheered on the writing of this book; to my mentors, Henry Steele Commager and Richard B. Morris; to Profs. Joanne B. Freeman of Yale University, Peter S. Onuf of the University of Virginia, Annette Gordon-Reed of New York Law School, Charles Zelden of Nova Southeastern University, and John Phillip Reid of New York University School of Law; to Maralyn Lowenheim, Gaspare J. Saladino, Michael A. Bellesiles, Felice J. Batlan, Benjamin Irvin, Barbara Wilcie Kern, Shalom Doron, Stephen and Stephanie Schechter, Ron and LaRae Carter, Marilee B. Huntoon, April E. Holder, Ron Blumer, Muffie Meyer, Ellen Hovde, Phillip A. Haultcoeur, Marvin Kitman, Hedy A. Lowenheim and Pat Wood, Mary E. P. Commager, Maureen K. Phillips, Joseph Newpol, Kathleen E. Spencer and Andrew MacLean (and their son, Aidan), Nathan D. Spencer and Jennifer MacLean (and their son, Evan), Edward D. Young III, Gina Tillman-Young, and their children, Christa, Adam, Noah, Luke, Peter, Mary Maya, and Moses.

Special thanks to the people who make Heights Books, Inc., and its sister store, Park Slope Books, a joy to visit (and work at) and an amazing resource: Ned Futterman (and his wife, Jeanine, and their children, Ben and Abigail), Stanley Fogel, Yuval Gans (and his wife, Vico), James Leopard, Marta Zïeba, Darcy Sharon, Amanda Brown-Inz, Monica Hairston, Emily J. Lordi, Erin Rogers, Richard Grundy, Alon Cohen, Jennifer Parkhurst, Harry Gonzalez, and above all Molly Myers.

PICTURE CREDITS

TEXT CREDITS

The texts of all documents in sidebars are drawn from Merrill D. Peterson, ed. *Thomas Jefferson: Writings.* New York: Library of America, 1984.

Page 18: Thomas Jefferson to John Harvie, January 14, 1760, p. 733.

Page 48: Declaration of Independence, July 4, 1776, pp. 19–24.

Page 59: Bill for Establishing Religious Freedom, pp. 346–347.

Page 148: Thomas Jefferson to Philip Mazzei, April 24, 1796, pp. 1035–1037.

Page 166: Thomas Jefferson, First Inaugural Address, March 4, 1801, pp. 492–496.

Page 169: Thomas Jefferson to Messrs. Nehemiah Dodge and Others, a Committee of the Danbury Baptist Association, in the State of Connecticut, January 1, 1802, p. 510.

Page 225: Thomas Jefferson to Roger C. Weightman, June 24, 1826, pp. 1516–1517.

R. B. Bernstein is adjunct professor of law at New York Law School and director of online operations at Heights Books, in Brooklyn, New York. He is the author or editor of 18 books on American constitutional history, including *Are We to Be a Nation? The Making of the Constitution* and *Amending America: If We Love the Constitution So Much, Why Do We Keep Trying to Change It?*, which were both nominees for the Pulitzer, Bancroft, and Parkman Prizes.